Et Libris

William J. Fay.

Covenant and Creation

Covenant and Creation

Piet Schoonenberg SJ

UNIVERSITY OF NOTRE DAME PRESS

First American Edition 1969
University of Notre Dame Press
Notre Dame, Indiana 46556

First Published 1968
Sheed and Ward Ltd., 33 Maiden Lane, London WC2, and
Sheed and Ward Pty. Ltd., 95 York Street, Sydney

Chapters 1–4 were originally published in *Het Geloof van ons Doopsel*,
vols. 1 and 2, L. G. C. Malmberg, 's-Hertogenbosch, 1955 and 1956

Nihil obstat: John M. T. Barton, S.T.D., L.S.S., Censor
Imprimatur: ✝Patrick Casey, Auxiliary Bishop of Westminster
            Vicar General
            Westminster, May 8, 1968

Library of Congress Catalog Card Number: 74-75119
Printed in the United States of America

Contents

Preface

Contemporary theology lends itself more to the writing of *quaestiones disputatae* than to the compilation of theological *summae*. I was not the first person to express this thought, though I have certainly experienced its truth for myself. Following the giving of a series of theological lectures for laymen in Amsterdam, I set myself the task of writing a dogmatics treatise. Like the lectures, this was to be built on the plan of the Apostles' Creed.

The title was *Het geloof van ons doopsel* (The faith of our baptism), which expressed my intention to explicate the faith into which we have been baptized, for us, the christians of today. In 1955 the first part appeared under the subtitle *God, Vader en Schepper* (God, Father and Creator), in which the first article of faith was dealt with. It was in no way my intention to write twelve volumes: I wished to cover the ground in six.

This plan has failed in various ways. The second, third and fourth parts each deal with only half the material I had meant to discuss in them. Because of this the task as a whole became increasingly protracted. However, since others made demands on me, my time become more and more limited. And there was another, all-dominating factor: the shift taking place in theology itself, a shift which is not yet complete. In the first volume I had already abandoned my original plan of merely broadening the Amsterdam course somewhat. For each part I have studied the material anew. In this way new questions presented themselves with each new volume. And these also concerned the parts already written. Such questions become more numerous for me in the measure that current theological thought is bringing about a 'shaking of the foundations'. For me these queries concern above all christology. I therefore intend to bring my dogmatics treatise to a close provisionally, without having completed it.

Meanwhile, the fourth part of my work, which presents a theology of sin—though I had intended to write a theology of the redemption—has drawn attention in wide circles, and this is particularly true of the theory of original sin it offers. An adaptation of this volume which gives, among other things, a more precise account concerning the relation between the 'sin of the world' and original sin, has appeared in English under the title *Man and Sin*. This book has been published by Sheed & Ward Ltd in London and by the Notre Dame University Press at Notre Dame, Indiana, USA. These publishers also made the suggestion that the previous parts of *Het geloof van ons doopsel* should, in so far as they are of current interest, be published in translation.

I have therefore selected several chapters from the first volume and a piece from the second dealing with miracles. From the first volume I have omitted a piece on man and the first man, which needs to be rewritten in the light of the theory of evolution. The remainder of the second part deals with the Old Testament as reference towards Jesus and with his messiahship and divine sonship in the books of the New Testament, but is traced exegetically. The third volume gives a speculative christology, which I should like to revise on certain points. For this reason I have only offered for translation the above-mentioned parts of volumes 1 and 2.

Verbond en schepping (Covenant and Creation) is the title I give to the book which has thus arisen. In fact the passages translated here all deal with these two subjects. It is not insignificant that the covenant is mentioned first, for in both testaments, above all in the old, God is first recognised as Yahweh, the God who has bound himself up with Israel as God of the covenant and God of history. Only in reflection upon this fact does God reveal himself as creator, so that it is only in a second chapter that Creator and creation are discussed. Subsequently, in a third chapter, we look back at the covenant from the viewpoint of the creation. The fourth chapter deals with the miracle, and once more much is said about creation and covenant.

The passages referred to were written a little over ten years ago. Time certainly runs on apace in theology, even for me, but in these chapters I nevertheless continue to recognise the foundations which still determine my thought today. This does not remove the possibility of their now being supplemented, and I shall make such an addition to this book in the form of an epilogue. The latter does not offer a complete treatment, but accompanies the reader along a path of thought that goes further. And that is precisely my intention: to make a contribution which stimulates further thought. For we have not only to conserve a doctrine, but also and above all to announce an inheritance of faith in a continually changing world. A tradition must be accepted, but it must also really be handed on to those who wish to listen to what the Spirit has to say to us today.

Introduction

In introducing this book it is perhaps best to start with an account of the circumstances which led to its being written. From 1951 to 1953 the author gave a course on the faith to intellectual lay catholics in Amsterdam. In doing this he decided to follow an extremely simple and clear plan, and chose that of the Apostles' Creed, sometimes known as the twelve articles of faith. Without detailed investigation of the various questions concerning the history and structure of this confession of faith, the content of each article was sketched, and a number of classes were devoted to elements of the faith which are not explicitly set forth in any one of the articles, but certainly presupposed by some of them, such as, for example, the doctrine on original sin. What has so far been said may already suffice to give the reader an idea of the contents of this book. We should now like to speak at greater length about the spirit of it and about the way in which we hope to treat our subject-matter; firstly by reflection on the public for whom we are writing, secondly by consideration of our title. First, therefore, a few words about those for whom we are writing, and then about the basis from which we have chosen to start.

1 *For whom has this book been written?*

The spirit and method of this book have been determined to a great extent by the lay audience mentioned above. It is not purely accidental, it seems to us, that this should be so. For we are of the opinion that the layman *must* play a part in determining theology, since layman and theology have need of each other. Certainly, it is generally accepted in theory, but not seen at all clearly enough in practice, that the catholic layman needs theology. He needs it not just in order to solve moral problems, but also, through his attitudes and their expression, to give a catholic witness in his world; above all, however, in order to maintain—or rediscover—within himself the balance between his profane knowledge and his christian life in order to find food for the latter which will make it blossom forth in prayer, in faith, hope and love. On the other hand, theology also needs the layman, if not as a specialist in it, then at least as partner in a dialogue. For every science, specialisation is equally a necessity and a danger. For theology the danger is that through this necessary and unavoidable specialisation—which we in no way wish to abolish, not even in terminology—it becomes separated from life, which in this context means separated from the appeal the church makes to the people of today so that they may hear in their own language God's great deeds. Who is there who does not see that this is a threat to the very existence of theology and, also, that dialogue with the layman—in the broadest sense—can avert this threat? And this not only through the production of a modern terminology or the directing of theology towards current problems. No, the theologian is forced by the layman to make the language and style of thought of his subject wholly comprehensible so as not only further to extend his affirmations, but also constantly to test them against their sources, so that in what—like every scientist—he builds up and constructs, he may still make manifest the original datum with its brilliance and first freshness.

From the above it will be quite clear that we find not just a certain part of theology important and necessary for the layman, but the whole of it. Not only a theology of the laity or of earthly realities which most intimately concern the layman, but the whole of theology, as far as that of the Holy Trinity and eschatology, is the food that he needs. In the same way, conversely, the layman is needed as a partner in a discussion for the treatment of the whole of theology. For the whole of revelation is meant for each and every christian, and every christian has not only to accept it in principle, but also as far as possible to think it out and make it effective in his life. And what has just been said of revelation holds also for theology, for its task is to do no less than interpret the whole of revelation; but also to do no more.

So far we have spoken of the layman only as the person whom we are addressing. From the spirit and method of treatment of our subject-matter, and in particular from the fact that this subject-matter covers the whole of theology, it will be evident that this book is in no way designed exclusively for the layman. The author would wish equally to say something at the same time to priests and religious, and he would even be pleased were a professional theologian to take a look at his work. In this connection, we should like to extend somewhat all we have said about the layman. The intention of this book seems to us best expressed by the following formula: *it addresses itself to all who wish to confess the ancient faith in the world of today*. It will already be clear, from what has been said earlier, that here the ancient faith and the modern world are not seen as mutually hostile powers which may only be brought together by means of concessions to one another, but rather as poles which determine each other. For the world of today asks its questions of faith, questions which compel the theologian to unearth the whole treasure of the faith and, particularly, to make visible the deepest roots of the latest growths.

The reader is perhaps now wondering what we mean in concrete terms by this and similar formulae, and wanting to see in this introduction a few more practical points concerning our programme. We shall try to satisfy his wish, although, naturally, only the book itself will give a complete answer to his question. Thus we will name one property which we should like to give to the expositions that follow, and that is a certain *completeness*. We say a 'certain' completeness, because as far as details are concerned we are not striving after completeness. What is intended, however, is a completeness with regard to essentials, the innermost convictions of our faith. We wish to uncover the great themes of revelation, and its internal coherence, whilst its justification in apologetics and its moral application will not be dealt with in this book, even though these may claim an importance of their own. In fact, we should like to achieve this completeness to some degree in each chapter. The first chapters would thus be intended to point to the fullness of the later ones, and in the later ones we would try to continually reach back to the first. Applying this now to our Apostles' Creed, we see that already in the acknowledgement of God, the father almighty, creator of heaven and earth, there is contained the whole of the history of salvation, up to and including its final development in the new heaven and the new earth, but also, conversely, that the first article will have to be constantly reconsidered as the Son and his incarnation and work of salvation, the Holy Spirit, the church and the resurrection are acknowledged. It is mainly in this way that we intend to discuss the twelve articles of faith, thus in such a way that this first part will only become manifestly complete in the following part, the acknowledgement of the Father in that of the Son and Spirit and church.

The most important points concerning the completeness we wish to achieve have now been covered. Another property, which is connected with the above one, may now receive mention. We wish, namely, to try to achieve completeness, catholicity with respect to all teachings and aspects of our faith. Obviously, this means that we shall try to avoid any heresy. Less obvious is our attempt to avoid falling into an attitude of defence which tries to evade the one-sidedness of heresy by a one-sidedeness in the opposite direction. For heresy—the word comes from the Greek *hairēsis*, meaning 'choice', 'partiality'—is a voluntary departure from full catholic truth, as indeed is every error and partial truth which is presented as the whole truth. To error, and particularly to heresy, our first word must thus be 'no', as is always the church's first reply. But our last word must never be simply the rejection of this partial truth which is presented as the whole truth, but rather the situating of it in the whole. We may not only not stand idly by in the presence of anti-protestantism, but there is also no excuse for doing nothing with regard to anti-humanism or anti-communism. On the contrary, in all rejection we must still let it be seen how the splintered truths of which these and other errors have made themselves masters are found more beautiful and powerful in the whole of catholic truth, which we were given entirely freely. Thus our exposition will contain, we hope, something of a dialogue not only with the needs, but also the tendencies and errors of today. In any case, we hope that fruits of catholic insight, which we believe we were permitted to obtain in conversation with protestant christians, will here and there be visible.

Someone reading this introduction may perhaps remark that we have a high estimation of dialogue. We began by recalling how the content of this book grew out of a course in which we were attempting a conversation with the layman, we continued by saying that we now have a broader intention, namely a dialogue with the whole of contemporary humanity, and we have concluded by expressing the hope that we should also be in dialogue with the mistaken tendencies of today. We do indeed have a high estimation of dialogue, and that as a source of knowledge; yes, we believe that knowledge unfolds itself there in one of its highest potentialities, because the self-communication of another person opens for everyone a richer source of knowledge than the 'interrogation' of mute objects (which, moreover, always goes together with dialogue between persons). The dialogue, the conversation, the meeting, however, is more than a revelation of knowledge alone, it is a blossoming of the whole person. For this reason we here express the wish that all these conversations between people may be joined, as the fruit of our reflection, by the highest and most important dialogue: the dialogue with God that is called prayer. We do not say this in order to be pious in addition to being theological. We wish to approach piety and prayer precisely through being theological, but theological in the sense we have described above. Here we may for a moment emphasise our resolve to penetrate to the sources and to the first freshness of revelation, by being as scriptural as possible. Not in a sense that excludes tradition and teaching authority, and which is *hairēsis*. But in the sense that scripture provides not just the material we use for our proofs, but the starting-point for the ideas we use and even, in a certain measure, for the system that may be discoverable in our writings. Here also it should be stressed that far from the least important aspect of the gift of the scriptures to the church is that they should nourish her life of prayer, as a source of praise and contemplation. Therefore we also write in the hope that, just as the bible has been the principal source of these reflections, so it may also become for the reader a source of life and prayer.

2 *The basis from which we have chosen to start*

The above consideration has already explained to our readers one of the words in the title of this work, namely 'Dialogues'. We write this considering external form, but inward disposition: dialogues in which people speak and listen, yes, listen while speaking, listening firstly to God's revelation in Christ, and then also listening to the ideas of contemporary man, so as to be able to proclaim in his language the great deeds of God. And with this we may proceed to the rest of our title, which speaks of faith, confession of faith, and baptism. We have already said that we chose the Apostles' Creed as a simple transparent plan. In fact, it gives clear divisions to the content of revelation; divisions, moreover, which do not depend upon a principle applied to it from without, but upon its own internal structure as self-communication of the three divine persons by their activity in the history of salvation. But there is another reason for having chosen the apostolic symbol of faith as our guide, and this lies in its relation to faith and baptism. This relation has many aspects. Naturally, this creed, like all the others, gives the content of God's revelation together with that of our faith, for the two are the same. But, in the Apostles' Creed, moreover, just as in other creeds connected with it, clear expression is given to the fact that everything that is confessed therein, is only asserted on the basis of the act of faith. It does not say: 'There is a God, the Father almighty', but: 'I believe in God, the Father almighty', and this first phrase 'I believe' governs everything that is further said in this creed. For anyone who is at all familiar with catholic teaching on faith, the reason for this may in no way be traced to a conception which would place the objectivity of the content of faith in brackets, but is only to be found in the all-dominating function of faith as the only way to the knowledge of what we confess, to the salvation that is proclaimed in that creed, and to the God of that salvation, the Father, the Son and the Holy Spirit. In this connection we can remember that the expression 'to believe in', *credere in aliquem* is specifically christian, and that it expresses orientation not primarily towards an object that is the content of faith, but towards a subject, a person, for whom and to whom one expresses oneself, to whom one consecrates and gives up oneself in faith and acknowledgement.

Now the relation which the apostolic formula has to the act of faith is the same as that which it at the same time has to baptism, since baptism is above all else an inward acceptance and outward confession of the faith. In saying this we naturally do not in any way deny that one can already have faith before baptism and that in this sacrament more is given than is denoted by our present-day term 'faith'. But sanctifying grace, hope, love and membership of the church, these also are all fruits of faith and thus the biblical term 'faith' often includes them all, whilst on the other hand faith, in the narrower sense it has in contemporary terminology, also reaches fulfilment and is expressed in the receiving of this sacrament. In former times this was seen more clearly than today. After each of the three questions (which still figure in our present baptismal liturgy) 'Do you believe in God, the Father almighty?', 'Do you believe in the Son?', 'Do you believe in the Holy Spirit?' and the affirmative answer 'I do believe', there took place a submersion of the neophyte, and this threefold submersion following the acknowledgement of each of three persons and their saving activity constituted the actual rite of baptism in the name of the Father, Son and Spirit. Now the Apostles' Creed contains the baptismal interrogation in its affirmative form. Thus it is above all a baptismal symbol of faith and can therefore be a continual reminder of the baptism in which we received the gift of this faith and expressed the acceptance of it by the whole of our being. When in her first two ecumenical councils, those of Nicea and Constantinople, the church for the first time made her faith in God the Son and God the Holy Spirit explicit in her baptismal creed (for the creed of our present-day mass is the elaboration of an earlier form of the apostolic formula), she was thereby repeating the call which Paul had made upon the Corinthians' acceptance of the faith: 'I would remind you, brethren, in what terms I preached to you the gospel, which you received, in which you stand, by which you are saved' (1 Cor 15: 1, 2a). The apostolic confession of faith reminds us of baptism in another more particular way, which we do not wish to leave unmentioned. The expression referred to above, namely, 'to believe in', *pisteuein eis*, finds a parallel in the likewise specifically Christian expression *baptizein eis to onoma*, 'to baptize in the name, or into the name' of the Father, the Son and the Holy Spirit. When we consider that there 'the name' is a semitic reference to the person himself, then it becomes all the more clear that both in baptism and in the act of faith there takes place the consecration and giving up of our being, of our human personality to the divine persons. This gift of one's personal existence to the God of our salvation, which is achieved once and for all time in our baptism and which, on the level of our intellect, is achieved in our faith, this gift of oneself is our basis in writing these dialogues on the Apostles' Creed. So let us say a little more about it.

For this we return once more to what we said about dialogue. Dialogue between people finds its deepest meaning not when it remains at the level of exchange of objective data which is in principle independent of the freely and personally determined existence of each of the participants, but when this existence, this personality, is unveiled, when there occurs a revelation and a meeting. Such a revelation, which really brings about the meeting with another person, in some degree presents our freedom with a decision: whether or not, faced by this self-revelation, to throw oneself open, whether or not to give oneself in a certain measure to the other, self-revealing person, whether or not to join with him in living community. If dialogue between human beings can bring about all this and achieve its highest development, if it brings about such a unity and is thence carried further, how much more is this the case when the word of God's revelation and the answer we pray become a dialogue. From the above description it should be clear to which form of human faith we should like to liken faith in the God of our salvation, divine faith, and its development will conclude our introduction.

Faith between human beings is always the acceptance of truths, but also, at the same time, a giving up of oneself to the person who is communicating them; to his authority, that is, to his capability, insight, reliability, and even to the care and love which makes him communicate his knowledge to us. This unlocking of the other person and the self-giving to him can sometimes to all intents and purposes disappear, namely when the witness of a whole crowd almost forces our agreement. As an example of this we would give belief in the existence of America, wondering at the same time whether here the acknowledgement together with the relevant witness is not a case of knowing rather than of believing. Faith between human beings appears in a much fuller sense when the authority, the value of the witnessing person or persons comes directly into question; when we trust in the capability of the investigator, in the discernment of the leader, in the intelligence, and even more so, in the intellectual honesty and the readiness of the messenger to serve the truth that is greater than he, or in the care and love which become immediately incarnate in the expression of it. The latter sort of personal disclosure, especially, explicitly faces those to whom it is directed with a free option to hand themselves over in faith, and this handing over of oneself in the act of believing is already, on the intellectual level, the beginning of a lasting community.

This last form of human faith, then, is the one to which we would liken divine faith first and foremost. We say 'first and foremost', because we think that here we must not be too ready to exclude. Even that form of human faith which relies on a massive witness of men has its resemblance to faith in the witness of God, in that through such a human witness error and deception are ruled out, and it holds true of God—though in an infinitely deeper and fuller sense—that neither he nor they can be mistaken or deceive us: *nec falli nec fallere potest* (Denzinger 1789).[1] Yet the guarantees of God's revelation never go so far that the acceptance of his revelation might be forced out of us or thrust upon us; on the contrary, man remains always free before the abundance of witness by Christ and his church. Hence his faith in this witness is in the end best likened to human faith in the leader, the friend, the beloved, although, precisely through God's truthfulness, divine faith is raised infinitely higher than these forms of faith between human beings. For these, whilst being the most personal, are at the same time by reason of our subjectiveness the most threatened forms of faith between men. Divine faith is indeed faith which 'believes the love God has for us' (1 Jn 4: 16) and it is thereby a decision to live in communion with him in his Christ.

In saying, then, that in this book we are going to talk about 'the faith of our baptism', we are expressing our intention to reveal all this richness in our dialogues. We intend, through the exposition of the content of the Apostles' Creed, to continually recall the memory of the all-deciding fact in the life of the Christian: baptism, a fact that can be described as more decisive than death. We recall the surrender of ourselves which took place at our baptism: the surrender to the God of our salvation, to the Father in Christ, which is fulfilled in faith, hope and love. Therefore we shall write with this decisive fact and this decisive attitude of the christian as our basis, not in an apologetic manner, but interpreting, yes, proclaiming a truth which is at the same time both a

[1] 'Denzinger' refers to K. Rahner's edition of H. Denzinger, *Enchiridion symbolorum, definitionum et declarationum de rebus fidei et morum*, Freiburg 1953[29].

promise and a fact, acknowledging an ascent to the Father through Christ, moved by the Holy Spirit. All this, however, must not be taken in a one-sided and mistaken way. We have already warned above that we do not intend to be pious apart from or in addition to being theological. Certainly we are not going in for straight apologetics, nor for moral theory—subjects, moreover, whose necessity and effectiveness we readily acknowledge—but we do certainly intend to provide dogmatic theology in an adapted form. Thus we are in no sense writing lyric, not even religious lyric, which is judged by its success in rendering the writer's own experience. Our norm remains always the sources of God's revelation —tradition and, above all, scripture, as we have explained—and that which may be read there by the believing mind in constant harmony with those sources and the whole of the believing thought of the church. Surrender to the Lord can only remain intact in a solid and accurate attachment to doctrine, for it is precisely in this that we meet him on the level of knowledge. Therefore we hope to couple clarity and solidity of rendering in these dialogues with the fullness and warmth of that surrender.

1
'God the Father almighty'

When, in our introduction, we described the completeness we wish to achieve in these dialogues on the Apostles' Creed, we also gave an idea of the manner in which we intend to consider the first article. For that completeness aims at seeing all there is to see in everything, at connecting each article with all the others, at the same time respecting that development of the theme which is shown by the structure of the creed itself. As we have already noticed, this implies on the one hand that the acknowledgement of the Father in the first article already presupposes that of the Son, Spirit, church and resurrection, while on the other the whole background of this first article is only fully manifest when we have considered the creed from first article to last. Hence we shall speak in very clear terms of God as he is acknowledged here in the first article, but leave in the background the most intrinsic quality of the Father's self-revelation, namely that its full meaning only breaks through in the revelation of Jesus Christ as Son of God. Here, then, we shall mainly sketch the Old Testament image of God and the way it introduces the revelation of God's fatherhood in Christ, only giving our full attention to the latter later, when we come to speak about 'Jesus Christ, his only Son, our Lord' and about ourselves as children of God through Christ in Spirit, church and forgiveness of sins. In the Old Testament, however, God seems to be preparing us for the New Testament revelation of himself as Father by his wanting to be a 'God-of', by the fact that he, who is without relations, wished to enter into and remain in relationship with man in the whole course of his history, and it is as such that we wish to talk about him in this chapter, drawing mainly, but not exclusively, upon the Old Testament.

1 *The God of the Covenant*

The first words of our first article are 'I believe'. All that will be said here about God is the confessing of a faith, although the necessary truths therein may also be detected by natural reason. When the First Vatican Council expressed its disapproval of conceptions of God which were certainly in the first instance philosophical errors, then in doing so it based itself on the faith of the church. Consider its majestic affirmation:

> 'The holy, catholic, apostolic, Roman church believes and confesses that there is one true, living God, the creator and Lord of heaven and earth, eternal, immeasurable, not able to be limited, infinite in intellect and will and all perfection; of whom it must be said, since he is a unique, perfectly simple and immutable spiritual substance, that in reality and by his essence he is distinct from the world, perfectly content in and of himself and ineffably higher than all that is or can be comprehended' (Denzinger 1782).

Given this faith, we must nevertheless point out that the content of our first article can partly and under a

2

certain aspect be perceived by man's own intellectual capacity, independently of God's revelation and the grace of divine faith. It can be known, as Vatican I puts it, 'by the natural light of the human reason' (Denzinger 1785). We say 'partly and under a certain aspect', because in the first place the very fatherhood of God in its real sense, as revealed in Christ, and also its preparation in the covenant-making activity of God under the Old Testament, fall outside that natural knowledge, and secondly, the existence, the attributes and the creative activity of God are more fully known by faith than by the reason alone. Nevertheless, man has a natural capacity of climbing to a knowledge of God.

Though the recognition of this capability is a point of faith that is expressly presented as such by Vatican I, the same council nevertheless adds that 'it is to be attributed to this divine revelation that that in the divine which is not inaccessible to the unaided human reason may, even in the present condition of the human race, easily and with firm certainty be known by all, without any admixture of error' (Denzinger 1786). In the domain of knowledge of God, the human reason cannot develop its powers fully and throughout all humanity because, whilst not being disabled, it is certainly fettered and mis-directed by sinful rebellion against the same God it strives to know. For this reason humanity's actual knowledge of God is the resultant of both this natural capacity and the sinful turning away. The human reason endeavours to unfold itself in affirma-tion of the infinite and personal God, but it would certainly seem that the influence of sin makes itself felt precisely in this, that the infinity and personal nature of God are seldom acknowledged together. The popular religion of paganism recognises a per-sonal God, but usually knows nothing of his infinity.

Thus it also accepts a multiplicity of gods, either as such (polytheism) or by allowing the possibility that other peoples may have other gods, while one adores a single god (henotheism). In general, monotheism occurs only in those speculations which try to rise above popular religion, as was the case with the neo-platonism and stoicism of the hellenistic world; but often what has thereby been gained in the way of insight into God's infinity has been lost in understanding of his personal nature. That is why this pagan monotheism often tends strongly towards pantheism and is certainly in itself more speculative than religious, and therefore also more tolerant of popular polytheism.

When God began in the Old Testament the revelation of himself which he was to complete in the New, he did not meet a human race which achieved its natural knowledge of God in the normal manner, nor one which was neutral with regard to this, but people who had fallen, even as regards their religious experience, into polytheism, namely people who 'exchanged the glory of the immortal God for images resembling mortal man or birds or animals or reptiles' (Rm 1:23). For God called Abraham from Ur of the Chaldees, where his fathers 'served other gods' (Josh 24:2; cf Judith 5:7ff.). The result of this intervention by God was the monotheism of Israel, which even from a historical point of view may be described as the most grandiose form of worship of one single God. Yet this monotheism of Israel differs radically from the pagan form sketched above. For in the first place, it did not grow through a gradual philosophical reflection, supported by political internationalisation, but arose by the very shock of God's intervention and was protected by Israel's separation from the heathen peoples. Furthermore, Israel's monotheism was neither speculative nor bloodless—

4

and far from tolerant—but did away with the gods and claimed the entire man for the sublime greatness of the almighty. And lastly and above all, this monotheism remained the service of a personal God, who wished, like the gods of the heathens, but in an infinitely deeper sense, to be a God of people, a God of covenant. It seems to us that if we elaborate these three points of difference in more detail, then the divine revelation of the Old Testament, the preparation of the New Testament revelation of God's fatherhood, will be outlined before us.

The origin and growth of Israel's monotheism

The monotheism of Israel arose through the shock of God's intervention, and through similar shocks it was also made more conscious. For the first shock did not make everything transparently clear. The story of Abraham in Gen 12–25 can, from its historical context, be explained in a number of different ways. Perhaps Abraham's journey out of Mesopotamia to the land of Canaan coincides with other migrations in the Near East at the beginning of the second millennium before Christ, just as later the journey of his descendants to Egypt and their sojourn there was part of a greater historical movement. But further—and more important—there are to be found, as regards religious experience itself, similarities between Abraham and his heathen surroundings. May we not compare the 'God of Abraham' to the gods of the other tribes? We can hardly believe it when we hear Abraham's grandson, Jacob, saying: 'The God of Abraham and the God of Nahor judge between us' (Gen 31 : 53; the 'Bible de Jérusalem' translates 'jugent entre nous', i.e., 'may they judge . . .'). However, this henotheistic formulation does not describe Abraham's faith in God completely, and certainly not when it is seen in the light of its continuation throughout the whole of the Old Testament. For, in the first place, from Abraham onwards God is the only One for Israel, in the sense that all polytheism is excluded from his cult, whence there appears a purity and a strength that are foreign to the henotheism of the surrounding peoples, as far as this exists. But also, God inwardly claims Abraham's whole person. He is the unique One, to whom he must give himself up in faith, hope and obedience. Abraham's human craftiness in trying to preserve his wife for himself comes to nothing through the circumstances, while Yahweh appears his only saviour. He must hope against all hope for the son promised to him, who in spite of Sarah's laughter is conceived and born, because: 'Is anything too hard for Yahweh?' (Gen 18: 14). Also, the story of the sacrifice of Isaac ordered and prevented by God rises, through Abraham's inward obedience, far above the description of a human sacrifice among the heathen. Thus from Abraham onward Israel's monotheism exists at the heart of experience, although it is only much later, with the advent of the prophets, that it finds its clearest expression.

Between these two phases, however, there lies another shock, that of the experience of Israel's salvation from Egypt. Here Yahweh is seen not only not to forget his people, but to save them, not only by destroying the earthly power of Pharaoh, but also by using the forces of nature for himself and by delivering up to his own people the peoples of Canaan, in spite of their gods. This second great experience of Israel makes monotheism fully explicit in the law and the prophets, and these latter will never tire of proclaiming that all the gods of all the nations are vanity, lies, filth and nothingness. Yahweh is, in the fullest sense, unique, and the proclamation of this will sharply distinguish Israel from each people with

6

which it comes into contact and from the whole heathen world. At the same time, then, it is clear from this how Israel's monotheism distinguishes itself from the speculative gentile monotheism not only by its explosive origin and its intolerance, but also by the fact that it did not grow out of a cosmopolitanism, but arose and remained in existence through Israel's separation. Considered under all these aspects together, it seems to us comparable only to the monotheism of Islam; but then this in its turn is partly dependent upon the Old Testament.

The God of holiness

Of more importance than this first characteristic of the monotheism of Israel are the two others, which we must therefore discuss more fully. Firstly, then, the way in which, as we said above, it is neither speculative nor bloodless, and far from tolerant, but does away with the gods and opens the whole person to the sublime greatness of the Almighty. This is already evident to some degree from what we have just said about the origin and preservation of Israel's divine faith. This greatness and transcendence of God becomes even more clear in a quality which Israel always attributed to Yahweh with most emphasis and in broadest measure, namely holiness.

We must now pause a moment to consider its meaning, doing this in the first place by looking at its occurrence in creation. Here someone or something is holy by his or its separation from normal—profane—human life for God and his worship. Thus the tabernacle and above all the 'holy of holies', where the ark is kept, are holy (Ex 25: 8; 26: 33); thus there is engraved upon the forehead-plate of the high priest 'holy to Yahweh' (Ex 28: 36), and the priests are consecrated to his service (Ex 28: 41;

29:44); yes, the whole people is chosen apart from the heathen nations in a special way for holiness to Yahweh (Ex 19:6). Therefore, as regards places, not just the tabernacle, but the whole camp is holy (Deut 23:14), while among the holy times and seasons, mention must be made in the first place of the sabbath (Ex 35:2; Gen 2:3).

All of this, however, is also seen among the heathens. But characteristic of God's revelation to Israel is the particular way in which the holy in creation is experienced. For it is not simply something negative, a separate and untouchable domain on its own, an impersonal 'taboo', but something especially appropriated by the personal God of Israel, filled with his presence and therefore also the place for his service, for meeting with him. In particular, the temple is filled with the cloud which enshrouds Yahweh's brilliant glory and indicates his benign presence, and it is thereby the centre, not of a mechanical ritual, but of prayer, its hearing and response. The particular nature of Israel's experience of God within the world of the holy appears still more clearly when its violation is punished: purely on the basis of objective happening and without any reference to inward guilt, yet not, on the other hand, by the automatic discharge of an accumulated amount of 'mana', but through Yahweh's wrath and his personal intervention, as when the ark is touched by Uzzah (2 Sam 6:7). We should already on this basis be able to establish that it is not man who is capable of making something or someone holy, but ultimately always God himself, and that through God's revelation this is no empty phrase for Israel but a living reality. This particular nature of the holy in Israel will become still more clear, however, as we now consider Yahweh's own holiness.

One of the most fundamental experiences of Yahweh's holiness is expressed in the vision in which Isaiah receives his calling and which finds a repeated echo in the New Testament both in John's Apocalypse and in the trisagion belonging to almost every christian liturgy. It takes place in the temple of heaven, which, in so far as it is perhaps considered as the idealisation or even the extension of the temple of Jerusalem, shows further correspondence to the Apocalypse and the eucharistic liturgy. In it Isaiah sees: 'Yahweh sitting upon a throne, high and lifted up; and his train filled the temple. Above him stood the seraphim; each had six wings: with two he covered his face, and with two he covered his feet, and with two he flew. And one called to another and said: "Holy, holy, holy is Yahweh of the hosts; the whole earth is full of his glory." And the foundations of the thresholds shook at the voice of him who called and the house was filled with smoke' (Is 6: 1–9). The holiness of God is not just the quality of being wholly-separate-and-other, but something active and positive. God is a ruler with a court, which consists of seraphim in Isaiah, of cherubim in Ezekiel, and of the 'sons of God' in the Book of Job and various psalms: thus, in short, of his angels. He himself also has his 'qabod', his might, his glory which here, as elsewhere, fills the earth. This is presented in scripture as thunder and lightning— mainly thus in the theophany of Sinai—but usually as a blinding flash of light tempered by the cloud that overshadows his sanctuary, or in the vision of Isaiah, by the smoke that fills it. The meaning of this majesty and holiness of Yahweh becomes clear from the attitudes of the seraphim in the vision: on the one hand there is the dread and awe with which they cover face and feet as if to disappear before God's omnipotence, just as the elders in the Apocalypse cast off their crowns and fall down before the throne. On the other, there is the jubilation which makes them shout forth, loud, strong, and continually, without resting day or night, as the Apocalypse says. What these seraphim are doing must also be man's reply to God's holiness and greatness; it is also the reply of the heavenly creatures in the Apocalypse. But here on earth man is in the first place so shocked by the sight of God that he must die. Thus Isaiah cries out during his vision: 'Woe is me! For I am lost; for I am a man of unclean lips, and I dwell in the midst of a people of unclean lips; for my eyes have seen the King, the Lord of hosts! Then flew one of the seraphim to me, having in his hand a burning coal which he had taken with tongs from the altar. And he touched my mouth, and said: "Behold, this has touched your lips; your guilt is taken away, and your sin forgiven"' (Is 6: 5–7). Man must be brought out of his unholiness to holiness, and only then may he approach God. But what is the nature of the holiness here required of man? When, just above, we described holiness within creation, we were considering objective holiness, ritual holiness, which is attributed to places, seasons, things, and also people, but people considered in their official position, their role in life. This is the holiness which is the opposite of the profane. With Isaiah, however, it seems rather to be a question of that holiness which may be described as subjective or, better perhaps, personal holiness, which arises through a man's inward attitude and personal option in life, and which is the reverse of sin. Isaiah's cry and the seraph's answer remind one of the psalm verse: 'Who shall ascend the hill of Yahweh? And who shall stand in his holy place? He who has clean hands and a pure heart, who does not lift up his soul to what is false, and does not swear deceitfully' (Ps 24 (23): 3,

4). Taken on its own, the 'guilt' and the 'sin' from which the prophet is cleansed may certainly be conceived of as a legal or ritual obstacle, comparable to Jeremiah's consecration before he left his mother's womb and by which he was destined to his role of prophet. In this context, however, a purely objective consecration in the vision of Isaiah's calling would seem unsatisfactory, because immediately after it he is sent out to give warning and announce punishments for truly inward sins. Indeed, one of the strongest accusations which he and the other prophets make against Israel is precisely that of observing ritual holiness and neglecting personal holiness. 'This people honour me with their lips, while their hearts are far from me', Yahweh says through Isaiah (Is 29: 13). With Jeremiah and Amos, Isaiah will place the cult in second place, with such emphasis that these prophets even seem to deny its value (Is 1: 10–15; Jer 7: 21ff.; Amos 5: 21–26). This will be above all done by Jeremiah through his prophecies of the approaching destruction of the temple (Jer 7 and 26), the focus of ritual holiness in Israel.

Thus we have returned from God's holiness to the holiness that exists within creation, and have defined the latter more clearly. But this also implies a clearer definition of God's own holiness, and we must make this explicit. Since, if Yahweh also requires personal holiness, it is clear that his holiness is a personal quality or attitude, which comes down to the fact that he 'loves virtue and hates sin'. This, being a biblical phrase, must be understood in its biblical sense, and not as if virtue and sin and thus holiness could have any meaning independent of God, to which he should conform. It is rather he who reveals himself as the original source of all the holiness that he requires of man, and this original holiness cannot be further expressed than in his requirements, his

judgement, and above all his attitude in the covenant with Israel, about which we shall speak
presently.

Now a few words about the separateness, the transcendence of God: that negatively expressed, yet so
positive aspect of God's holiness which we noticed
first. This also is revealed more clearly in the
measure in which Yahweh makes, through his prophets, higher demands as regards inward holiness. In
heathen religious experience it remains possible that
in spite of all affirmations of God's separateness his
presence, and thereby perhaps also his existence,
still remains bound to the places consecrated to him:
compare how Naaman wants to take earth with him
from Israel to Syria so as to worship Yahweh upon
it (2 Kings 5: 17). Now this is impossible for Israel.
Yahweh is independent of all that manifests him to
his people. Elijah experiences his presence not in the
Sinaitic phenomena of storm, earthquake or lightning, but in a soft breeze (1 Kings 19: 11ff.). Above
all, however, Yahweh is seen to be independent of
his temple in Jerusalem and of the worship offered
to him there. For Yahweh himself fulfils the above-
mentioned prophecies of Jeremiah through 'Nebuchadnezzar, his servant', to manifest himself thereafter in the land of exile to Ezekiel, far from the
ruins of his temple, accompanied by cherubim in
place of seraphim and surrounded by symbols of his
power of omnipresence (Ezek 1). 'Such was the appearance of the likeness of the glory of the Lord.
And when I saw it, I fell upon my face, and I heard
the voice of one speaking. And he said to me: "Son
of man, stand upon your feet, and I will speak with
you"' (Ezek 1: 28–2: 1). These words underline the
transcendence, the inaccessibility, the incompara-
bility of God already indicated by the prophet's

constant use, in describing his vision, of 'as it were' or 'the likeness of . . .', and his never clearly depicting its content. We find the overwhelming element in God's appearance to the 'son of man' once more in the prophet Daniel (Dan 7 : 9; 10 : 7–9).

It may be said that this aspect of infinite transcendence will dominate the post-exilic image of God. The traditional name of the God of the covenant, 'Yahweh', is suppressed by paraphrases such as 'the angel of Yahweh'. There arose the custom of reading 'Adonai', 'the Lord', in its place, whilst expressions such as 'The lord or king of heaven and earth' and paraphrases such as 'heaven' or 'the heavens' come more and more into fashion. The Babylonian crisis leaves behind a Jewish community for whom all idolatry is foolishness (Wisdom 13) and which rigidly maintains its monotheism; although here again a magic of their own temple, but above all of the law, can find a place, as the reactions of the New Testament will demonstrate. For the Jewish community God has indeed become an infinitely exalted, incomparable, incalculable sovereign. Everything is in his hand, he is the creator of everything (we shall study this more closely in a further chapter) and therefore God's commands and decrees to man are not to be understood, only to be worshipped. This is expressed in a flood of imagery in the two addresses of Yahweh to Job (Job 38–41). 'Who is this that darkens counsel by words without knowledge? Gird up your loins like a man, I will question you, and you shall declare to me. Where were you when I laid the foundation of the earth? Tell me, if you have understanding. Who determined its measurements—surely you know! Or who stretched the line upon it?' (Job 38 : 2–5). We end our description of God's holiness with this piece of divine irony that overwhelms the man Job. In it most emphasis is given to the transcendence that is always seen in this holiness.

The God of the covenant

With the rise of Israel's monotheism, however, and the holiness and transcendence of God that it acknowledges, we still only have half the divine revelation of the Old Testament, and the remaining part is that which most directly prepares the New Testament revelation of God's fatherhood. This preparation consists of God's wanting to be a 'God-of', the God of Abraham, Isaac and Jacob, the God of Israel, so as to finally reveal himself as 'the God and Father of our Lord Jesus Christ'. Already through his creation, God can be called 'God of something': thus he is 'the God of heaven' (Gen 24: 7, *passim* in later books such as Ezra and Nehemiah, and in Dan 2), 'the God of heaven and of the earth' (Gen 24: 3). Here, however, the preposition 'of' does not yet refer to a covenant that God has made, but rather to the pure initiative from God's side and the pure dependence of the creature, as we shall explain in the following chapter. Thus it may be more correctly said that it is creation that is of God: 'the earth is the Lord's' (Ex 9: 29), 'earth is the Lord's and the fullness thereof' (Ps 24 (23): 1). Yet in holy scripture as a whole this creator-creation relationship is rarely expressed by adding the preposition 'of' to God or the earth. Much more often Yahweh is the God of the fathers and of Israel, and Israel is Yahweh's people. Here even possessives are used. For not only is Israel 'his people', 'your people', but also God himself 'is not ashamed to be called their God' (Heb 11: 16). If in some place the relationship of creator to creation is expressed by calling God 'God of heaven and earth' and in others by saying that the earth is 'Yahweh's', in others still the two relations are

14

placed side by side in order to characterise the covenant. Already God says to Abraham: 'I am your shield' (Gen 15:1); in his turn, Abraham must 'walk before God' (Gen 17:1). This reciprocity is expressed in reciprocal achievement: God gives fertility, Abraham and his house circumcise themselves (Gen 17). To Jacob God says: 'I am Yahweh, the God of Abraham your father and the God of Isaac' (Gen 28:13). And from then on he is 'the God of Abraham, Isaac and Jacob', or simply 'the God of your fathers'. He will show himself thus to Moses in the burning bush (Ex 3:6) when he fulfils for the children the promises of the covenant which he made to their fathers. When he has done this, he will say: 'I am Yahweh, your God, who brought you out of the land of Egypt, out of the house of bondage' (Ex 20:1). But the fruit of Yahweh's covenant with Israel is not only a liberation, it is also a lasting presence, which we find expressed thus in Leviticus: 'And I shall make my abode among you, and my soul shall not abhor you. And I will walk among you, and will be your God, and you shall be my people' (Lev 26:11, 12). The Old Testament repeats this most pregnant covenant formula a number of times, in particular to express the new and eternal covenant (Jer 31:33; Ezek 37:27; Zech 8:8) and the New Testament also sees it confirmed, once with reference to the church on earth (2 Cor 6:16) and once for the heavenly Jerusalem (Rev 21:3). So, from Abraham and Moses on, but above all in Christ, God is characterised as the God of his people, as their God, or rather 'our God', who will further reveal himself as 'our Father'.

What this means in the biblical revelation of God can be determined by pointing firstly to those attributes which particularly characterise him in the exercising of his covenant. Thus we shall do better to speak of his 'personal attitudes' in this covenant. Let us name two which are repeatedly mentioned together, particularly in the Psalms, namely Yahweh's 'steadfast love and faithfulness', his *misericordia et veritas*. Not just faithfulness, but 'grace', 'steadfast love'—*hesed*—is also used in the Old Testament for a relationship between people. Here it can be described as: loyalty in fulfilling a contract, a loyalty that exceeds strict legal obligations. Thus *hesed* may be rendered as 'kindness' when it is an attitude, and 'favour' when a deed. David and Jonathan ask such a *hesed* of each other in the moving encounter of 1 Sam 20. So also with Yahweh himself; his *hesed* is, in its most original sense, the fulfilling of his covenant with Israel, just as, conversely, the faithfulness of man to the covenant with Yahweh is also *hesed* and he himself is thereby a *hasid*, a 'just one'. On various occasions, then, Yahweh's grace is connected with the exodus and the covenant (Ex 15: 13; 20: 6; 34: 6; Deut 7: 9; 1 Kings 3: 6; Is 54: 10; Ps 89 (88): 2, 3, 15, 25; Ps 100 (99): 5; Ps 106 (105): 1; Ps 107 (106): 1; Ps 117 (116): 2; Ps 136 (135); etc.). This *hesed* also reveals itself, however, when men are unfaithful (as early as Num 14: 18–20), and so the actual meaning of our words 'grace' and 'mercy' emerges, partly due to the Septuagint translation *eleos* (Vulgate *misericordia*) and its predominance in the New Testament.

A personal attitude which equally characterises Yahweh as God of the covenant is his 'truth' or 'faithfulness'. Both these words approach the one Hebrew word *emet*, which signifies that something or someone is steadfast, unshakeable, so that they may be relied upon, counted upon, and also that this is the only reality with which one has to reckon and upon which one must therefore build. This may sometimes be rendered by 'truth', but only in the measure that one must attribute to the Septuagint word *alētheia* and *veritas* in the Vulgate the above described fullness of meaning of the Hebrew term, rather than just the Greek sense of 'lying-open for in-sight', not being concealed (*a-lētheia*). God's truth is certainly not that of a timeless world of ideas which lies concealed behind irrelevant phenomena, it appears rather in his saving historical activity, primarily in the liberation from Egypt and the making of the covenant. Thus the *emet* of Yahweh is at various times connected with these facts, and also mentioned in the same breath as his *hesed* (Ex 34: 6; Deut 7: 9; Ps 89 (88): 3, 15, 25; Ps 100 (99): 5; Ps 117 (116): 2). 'Love and faithfulness' are thus the classic qualities which are attributed to Yahweh as God of the covenant. Through the context of Israel's desertion, *hesed* came more and more to have the meaning of love, mercy towards sin, *misericordia*, *eleos*. Similarly, God's faithfulness shows itself more and more as eternal faithfulness as opposed to the unfaithfulness of the partner in the covenant. Israel, thus as merciful faithfulness, as eternal love. Because of this Yahweh remembers his people yet again after raging against them, because of this—after the breaking of the old covenant—for the sake of sinners he raises the prospect of a new and eternal covenant.

This thought of eternal love and eternal covenant is found in Jeremiah (31: 3, 31–37; 33: 20–26), and also in the striking comparison in the Deutero-Isaiah: 'can a woman forget her sucking child, that she should have no compassion on the son of her womb? Even these may forget, yet I will not forget you' (Is 49: 14). Yahweh's loving faithfulness in the face of Israel's unfaithfulness is indeed the great theme of all the prophets, and very expressly that of the Song of Solomon. This most profound expression of God's love in the Old Testament (which we are accustomed to calling the law of fear . . .) already closely approaches Saint John's summary of God's saving activity in the new covenant: 'In this the love of God was made manifest among us, that God sent his only son into the world, so that we might live through him. In this is love, not that we loved God but that he loved us and sent his son to be the expiation for our sins' (1 Jn 4:9, 10). We shall later speak about this sending of God's son and of his work of reconciliation. Here we hope to have already given an image of God as the God of the covenant, primarily by naming some of his qualities or personal attitudes.

We say 'primarily', for we should now like, in a closer study, to try to make clear the degree to which this image of the God of covenant dominates the whole divine revelation of the Old Testament. Let us touch upon a few points. From the various descriptions of God—excepting perhaps the prohibition of the making of an image of him—there seems to be little concern about stressing that he is a spirit; no, the whole emphasis falls on the fact that he is a personal God. We might almost say: a God of interpersonality. God's spiritual nature is something that is only implicitly experienced by Israel. On the level of explicit description, in fact, we find that parts of the human body are attributed to him: he frees his people from Egypt with outstretched arm, there is talk over and over again of his face, and Moses sees Yahweh's back (Ex 33:23). On closer inspection, however, we find that the bodily form of Yahweh is never described in its entirety—this strikes one particularly in the above-mentioned visions of Isaiah and Ezekiel—except perhaps in the Song of Solomon 5:10–17 (at least, according to the directly allegorical interpretation), yet even here Yahweh is not directly mentioned by name and it is in general the handsomeness of the beloved that is praised rather than his appearance that is described. We think, therefore, that one can say that the attribution of bodily parts may perhaps say nothing against a possible corporeity of God, but also nothing in its favour. These anthropomorphisms rather serve the description of Yahweh's personality in the covenant. His outstretched arm signifies the force with which he works and fights for his people. The appearance of his form occurs in order to call and to send. Seeing Yahweh's back indicates the incapability and unworthiness of man to behold his face. But it is particularly his face that represents him in his wrath and above all in his kindness, in short, in his personal relationship with Israel and with separate individuals from the people of his covenant. Just as in interhuman relationships, the face is that part of the body which plays the most expressive part in encounter between persons.

There is yet another anthropomorphism which exists in this connection, namely the one which attributes not only human emotions, but also changes of emotion to Yahweh. It is a general theme of the prophetic view of Israel's history that Yahweh's wrath is set alight by the unfaithfulness of the people, but that at Israel's repentance Yahweh himself also repents of his earlier anger. Here also it should be noticed that this in no way signifies an intention of humanising the image of God; consider, for example, the mention of Yahweh's repentance concerning Saul's selection and the remark in the same chapter, 'He is not a man, that he should repent' (1 Sam 15: 11, 29). It is much more the case that all these changes of feeling in God's reaction to the attitude of Israel, just as the various expressions according to which he is 'provoked' by sin and reconciled by conversion, refer to Yahweh's dialectical activity, his living with Israel, his being a partner in the covenant, as this is developed in the course of history.

However, it is not only Yahweh's changing attitudes, but also his constant ones that are understood very much in terms of the covenant; thus not only the 'love and faithfulness' mentioned above, but others also. Their content is either determined to a vast extent by the covenant or recognised only in its execution, and all of this in a way that is astonishing to our mode of thought. Thus we habitually think of God's righteousness or justice as rewarding goodness or punishing evil. For Israel the retribution of evil is very much in the background, at least in connection with this attribute of Yahweh; it is above all through the keeping of his promises, and thus by coming to the aid of his people and the just to save them from oppression, that he is just (Ps 5: 9; 9: 2–21; 35 (34): 24; 71 (70)). This even in spite of the sins of men, so that Yahweh is entreated, because of his justice, not to enter into judgement, for no one is righteous in his sight (Ps 143 (142): 2). So the justice of God is an example of an attribute whose content is for the most part determined by the covenant. An example of what is perhaps an absolute attribute of God, but which is perceived almost only in the carrying out of the covenant, is that of God's eternity, about which we shall speak in the following section. We could continue our consideration of other attributes of God as functions of the covenant and we should then perhaps have to say the same about God's omnipotence; but we now intend to sum everything up by talking about the name that indicates his essence, the name 'Yahweh'.

In God's first appearance to Moses, the theophany of the burning bush, this divine name of given the meaning of 'I am who I am' (Ex 3 : 14), and in this is followed the practice of popular etymology customary in sacred books. It is generally accepted that an unlimitedness in Yahweh's being is expressed by this interpretation of the name. However, the question is: what is the exact content of this 'being'? It seems to us that no better answer can here be given than by understanding this again in terms of the covenant. God is there for Israel, his being is an aiding presence, a being together with his people, a divine *Mitsein* (being together with); with all these terms understood in the full sense they have in contemporary existential-philosophical terminology. It is precisely for this reason that God's affirmation concerning his name is the crowning of his promise to free Israel from Egypt, that from Egypt onwards God is called 'Yahweh' and that after the passage through the Red Sea Moses can summarise all aid and salvation by saying 'Yahweh is his name' (Ex 15 : 3). Yahweh's name signifies that for Israel, as for its fathers, he is strength, renown, rock, 'my protecting trust'. Thus the name 'Yahweh' denotes all the attributes we have discussed, and shows him *par excellence* as the God of the covenant.

Thus we have not only drawn Yahweh as God of the covenant, but have also tried to show the place of this idea in the divine revelation of the Old Testament, the way in which it characterises this revelation. Finally, we should like to develop this further by comparison with the image of God that our natural reasoning is capable of producing. Our reason can arrive by its own illumination at a monotheism, but at the same time it is only freed in its fallen state by grace, so as to develop itself naturally and normally. Let us compare some of the features of this monotheism of *theologia naturalis* with the monotheism of Old Testament theology such as is marked out mainly by the idea of the covenant. If we limit ourselves to the affirmation of Yahweh's holiness which we discussed above, then little difference is evident. For in this holiness we rediscover God's transcendence on the level of religious representation. A complete elaboration of this transcendence is not to be found in the Old Testament, although enough of its elements are indicated. The same is true of all God's absolute attributes, as we have already demonstrated with respect to his eternity. What do we find in Old Testament divine revelation, however, of the relative attributes from natural theology, of God's activity outside his essence? Here the natural reason places God's creative activity first, the activity to which all his other activities may in a certain sense be reduced; thus, to sum up: his basic causality with respect to the whole of finite reality. This creative activity of God is acknowledged with great emphasis in the Old Testament, but takes second place behind God's covenant activity, as we shall see in the following chapter. For Israel Yahweh is first and foremost God of the covenant, and only thereafter creator God.

The question may now be put: is the Old Testament image of God in this inferior to an ideal natural conception of God? At first sight one is inclined to say that it is. For we have seen that God's activity in carrying out the covenant is in broad measure represented anthropomorphically, and we know in addition that the heathen gods were also gods of covenant; examples are Kamosh the god of Moab, and Marduk the god of Babel. On the other hand, however, we noticed that these anthropomorphisms in no way indicate a humanisation of God. It was noticed at the same time in the description of Yahweh's holiness that his transcendence was experienced from the very beginning and throughout the history of the covenant, and that it was later explicitly acknowledged. If, therefore, an inferiority of Old Testament theology is asserted, this is but an appearance that must be overcome. We do not hesitate to state that behind this appearance the Old Testament surpasses natural theology in reality, in as much as it is a *super*natural theology, as we shall see later. With our reason we know God as having no relativity at all, and this remains true. When we think of him in relation to the world, then this relation is without any dependence, while on the contrary, the world is completely and utterly dependent on God's total causality, from which all initiative proceeds. What has been said here about God as regards perfection also holds true of revelation, as is already clear from the summary of his creative activity: 'He spoke, and it came to be' (Ps 33 (32): 9; Judith 16: 17). Over and above this, however, revelation refers to a perfection of God which, in the absence of this revelation, we should only be able to conceive of as an imperfection and attribute to him in an anthropomorphic way. God acts not only in creating, namely, but also dialectically. Not only is the full initiative with him, he presupposes at the same time the personal nature of his creature, and 'asks' and 'awaits' the latter's reply. He is not limited to being purely cause and initiative, he is not imprisoned in his creative activity, but the activity of dialogue, which in us always goes hand in hand with dependence, humility, imperfection, is also in him, but as perfection. The anthropomorphisms of the Bible which we mentioned are therefore not only necessary in order to approach God's essence in a culture which was not yet capable of forming the purified concepts of our metaphysical theology, but also, and above all, in order to make known that perfection which can never be expressed in our metaphysical ideas. The prophets are certainly no pre-cursors of later philosophy, but complete and sur-pass this on a supernatural level. And the revelation of the burning bush does not provide a popular description of *esse a se* (being of itself alone), but exceeds this idea by far. In this much, to use Pascal's famous remark, the God of Abraham, Isaac and Jacob is not the God of the philosophers. In the doctrine on creation, on the Holy Trinity and in many other places we shall be obliged to return to this fundamental distinction. We hope then to justify it by a further elaboration, and for this reason we trust that it is enough to have announced this theme here.

We have now completed our treatment of the three elements by which Israel's monotheism is distin-guished from every other monotheism. These were: origin and growth through sudden intervention by God, through God's utter holiness and transcend-ence and, above all, through his covenant. Though we are not going any further into the origin and growth, we can see the nature of Israel's monotheism marked out clearly by the two other points, God's holiness and his covenant, taken together. Therefore it seems desirable to finish our description of the divine revelation of the Old Testament by once more considering these two aspects of God's nature together, and by showing how on the one hand his holiness relates itself to the covenant, and on the other, in his love for the people of the covenant, he remains always the Holy One. It may be noticed in passing that his holiness is also directed towards the covenant. God's holiness inspires fear, but is not repulsive, his throne above the clouds brings no lack of concern about his people on earth. He is rather 'the Holy One of Israel', 'the Holy One in your

24

midst, who will not come to destroy' (Hos 11:9). Like the idea of God's righteousness, so also that of his holiness is influenced by the covenant.

Fuller mention must be made of the fact that in the love of his covenant, Yahweh still maintains his requirement: 'be holy, for I am holy' (Lev 11:44; 19:2; 20:7). Yahweh's love is that of the infinitely great one, and it is therefore also infinitely demanding: it demands everything. The Old Testament expresses this by saying that Yahweh is a jealous God: 'Yahweh, whose name is Jealous, is a jealous God' (Ex 34:14; cf Ex 20:5; Josh 24:19; Ezek 39:25). On account of this jealousy he wants Israel to remain true to him and thus not to go after any strange gods, this not only by not abandoning Yahweh's service, for even the serving of other, lesser gods besides him is an abomination to him: here we have the unique intolerance of Old Testament monotheism. 'How long will you go limping with two different opinions? If Yahweh is God, follow him; but if Baal, then follow him' (1 Kings 18:21). The first commandment forbids the having of any other gods 'besides Yahweh' (Ex 20:3; 34:14–16). This first commandment is formulated in a completely intimate and positive way in Deuteronomy, where it is preceded by the first article of Israel's monotheistic faith: 'Hear, O Israel: Yahweh is our God, Yahweh alone; and you shall love Yahweh your God with all your heart, and with all your soul, and with all your might' (Deut 6:4, 5). With this we are standing at the edge of the New Testament once more. We there hear Jesus himself take over this formula from Deuteronomy in his statement about the first and greatest commandment of the law (Mt 22:37; Mk 12:30; Lk 10:27). He also takes over the rejection of duplicity in his famous remark: 'No one can serve two masters; for either he will hate the one and love the other, or he will be devoted to the one and despise the other. You cannot serve God and money (Mammon)' (Mt 6: 24).

Thus we end our description of Old Testament divine revelation with a look at the New Testament, which is logical, since the first article of the Apostles' Creed also acknowledges the revelation of the New Testament. Let us conclude by pointing out how everything that is said in the New Testament about God summarises or presupposes his holiness and his covenant relationship. This is already the case with the 'kingdom of God', that basic idea in Jesus' preaching in the synoptics, about which we shall have to speak in more detail later. Let it be noticed here, however, that this kingdom is the situation in which God's jealousy is completely and utterly satisfied, in which his name is hallowed and his will done, in which he is indeed loved *ex toto*, with the whole self, in which he is 'everything to everyone' (1 Cor. 15: 28). This presupposes God's holy majesty, but equally his being a God of covenant, for this kingdom is not present from the beginning of creation, purely, in other words, through the fact that God spoke and it came to be. No, it comes about through his reign being assented to in the obedience, service, sacrifice and love of human beings, which is also the reason why only those who do the Father's will shall enter into his kingdom (Mt 7: 21). However, not only are God's holiness and his covenant relationship presupposed by the idea of the 'kingdom of God', we also hear them both in various of God's descriptive titles. At the time of Jesus the holy awe of God's name had developed so far that the name 'Yahweh' was paraphrased by 'the Lord' (*Adonai*), or one spoke of 'the Mighty One' (see Lk 1: 49) or 'the Lord of heaven', or also 'the heavens' (whence the expression 'the kingdom of heaven' in

Matthew). Now, very often both Jesus himself and his apostles take care to let this respect be heard in the reference to God as Father. Thus the Lord teaches us to pray: 'our Father, who art in heaven' (Mt 6:9), and he himself, rejoicing in the Holy Spirit, says: 'I thank thee, Father, lord of heaven and earth' (Mt 11:25; Lk 10:21). The apostles prefer not simply to take over the title of Father for God, but speak repeatedly of 'our God and Father', 'the God and Father of the Lord Jesus' (2 Cor 11: 31). Finally, we find these two aspects of God's single nature once more in the formulation of our own first article of faith: 'I believe in God, the Father almighty.' Here, then, we end this first section on the Father as God of the covenant.

2 *The God of history*

God, as we said in the introduction to this chapter, God who is without any relativity, wanted to enter into and remain in relationship with humanity in the whole course of its history. His relationship to man, his covenant with a people, we have described in the previous section. We should like now to try to throw further light upon the way in which at the same time God thereby fully enters into the history of his people and that of the whole of humanity, and may thus rightly be called a God of history. As in the previous section, we may begin with a summary comparison between judaism and christianity on the one hand, and the remaining religions on the other. After this we shall be able to take a closer look at what it means for God to be a God of history. Still following the plan of our treatment of the first article of faith, we shall for the most part introduce the subject in the present section, using the Old Testament as our main but not exclusive source. Just as in the preceding section the

27

image of God was described without deliberately involving the revelation of his fatherhood in the appearance of his Son, so here also we shall not yet proceed from God's most basic intervention in history through the incarnation of that Son. Thus not all of its consequences will be made manifest, although we shall necessarily mention them.

The revelation of history

Man has a history not only as regards his body, but also as regards the expression of his mind in and through his physical aspect. It is not as a biological entity that man has a history. Just as the evolution of species of plants and animals can hardly be called history in the full sense of the word, so we should not use the same word to refer to the development of the human body in different races. No, it is the unique human person, such as he asserts himself in his free decisions, which forms history. Here we are in no way saying that necessity and above all community are absent in history. On the contrary, it is precisely those situations within the whole of humanity or within its constituent communities which arise from personal decisions, and conversely, decisions that may be explained in terms of given situations (without injury to freedom): it is this interaction between decision and situation, and thereby of freedom and necessity in the community, that forms history. Now when God, as we saw in the previous section, enters into covenant and community with man, this at the same time implies that he participates in this interaction. Thus he is not only the writer or producer of the drama of human history, but also a player in it. Or, to put it the other way round, he is the leading actor, without anything being thereby taken away from his complete dominion, just as he is also God of covenant and holy

28

ruler precisely because of this, as he is at the same time Father and almighty.

In the above, proceeding from human history, the idea of the God of history has been sketched out in a few lines. And yet man does not have this idea in or of himself, but through the free entry of God into his history. As far as the natural human reason is concerned, the subject of this section has an inaccessibility which, it appears to us, is most clearly perceived when compared to the inaccessibility of what we described in our last section. The God of the covenant, the God of Abraham, Isaac and Jacob, as we there described him, is not the God of philosophy, and it would even be impossible for him to be so, because this covenant is free gift, is supernatural. However, his titles of God of the fathers and of Israel express the fact that he is God of history in the same concrete way as he is God of the covenant. Neither can this be found by our natural reason, and herein lies the first element in the inaccessible character of our present subject which corresponds to one of the previous section. But there is yet another. In addition to the above, outside his revelation and thus outside the covenant with him, complete detection simply of the existence of the one true God by humanity is to a great extent hardly possible. Such is also the case with the existence, pure and simple, of history. As we indicated above, as interaction between situation and decision, outside the history of salvation it remains to a great extent withdrawn from the human eye, indeed, the truth concerning it is even suppressed or hindered (Rm 1 : 18). Just as in the previous section, we must not proceed from a recently obtained conception of human history in describing the revelation of the God of history, but from the gentile who, in many respects, is without history, because he is 'without hope and without God in the world' (Eph 2: 12). Here also we must start in Ur of the Chaldees, where 'your fathers served other gods' (Josh 24: 2).

Now the man we find in the world into which God's revelation has not yet penetrated is to a large extent a man who in his conscious life stands outside history. He has precisely no full awareness of the situation and above all of personal decision in its uniqueness, and is thus not alive to the definitive and unrepeatable character of history. On the contrary, he is imprisoned in the endless repetition of biological process and therefore conceives of the whole of human existence, with relations to the divine world included, as imprisoned in the cyclic movement of an ever-new rejuvenation and endless return. This presupposes that everything has a divine or mythical primeval type; not only the world as a whole, but also the building of towns and houses, marriage, hunting, farming, navigation and even war; everything was founded and inaugurated by an act of gods or heroes. Proceeding from this assumption, the positive aspect of ahistoricism is found in this, that these primeval types are continually imitated, these mythical deeds become reality over and over again in their celebration and imitation, and thereby everything is renewed; all withering away, wear, decay and guilt is done away with. For primitive man, not only is the building of a house or entering into marriage an identifying imitation of a primeval divine act and thereby a new creation, but even every year has this character.

This suppression and negation of the definitive and unrepeatable nature of history is not, however, the exclusive property of primitive, prehistorical, pre-socratic man. It also remains in most great historical cultures. As is to be expected, in the first place this mythical, ahistorical mentality lives on in the substratum of these civilised peoples. However, it is remarkable that in those peoples among them which make and experience history intensely, this history is still interpreted on the basis of a historical, cyclic thought, so that this latter continues to dominate the official religion, mythology and political doctrine. Thus the kings become sons of the deity, saviours and renewers. This mostly in the Far and Near East, naturally, but it is precisely a characteristic of hellenistic–Roman culture that this eastern element pervades it together with an abundance of mystery religions, which spread on a wide scale the primitive ahistorical experience of renewed rebirths. It is in India, however, that this cyclic experience predominates in the most universal way and is raised to the level of a system. Here it forms the main content of hinduism, as also the basic presupposition and point of departure of buddhism in its different forms. Not only is human life doomed here to recommence through constantly returning rebirths, but in the first place the whole cosmos is shut up in aeons which are represented as greater and greater as time goes by, but which are continually affirmed anew and which are constantly beginning with a new dawn and a golden era, then to progress to downfall along an ever-steeper decline, so that they end in a total chaos—and then begin again, following the same rhythm. Over and against this, Greek thought after Socrates showed itself philosophical by its (relative) distance from myths and sacred books; but the primitive experience of reality left clear traces in it. These are to be seen in the mythical interest in the archetypal blood, expressly in Plato's theory of ideas and as a background to the whole dispute concerning universal concepts. But also the period of the 'great year' with its general decline, the *metakos-mēsis*, and its renewal, and the *apokatastasis* appear with Plato, to pervade the hellenistic schools of philosophy from his time onwards. With this is connected Virgil's philosophy of history, in which the expectation of an end to Rome and to the world is replaced by belief in the renewal of both by Augustus and his empire of peace—a belief, however, that was unable to stand up against the threatening decline of the Rome of the emperors. Thus we hope to have shown in broad outline the ahistorical cyclic conception of time which man has without revelation, whether he be prehistorical or conscious of history.[1]

If to the above we now oppose the historical conception of time of the man who has been reached by revelation—even though he may have repudiated this contact and thereby secularised his recognition of history—then this opposition must not be conceived of as absolute. For the man outside revelation does not ipso facto have to deny every sort of definitive ultimate situation, and certainly not as regards the individual. Whether he actually affirms such a definitive final state of the world, however, remains a question. Virgil's eternal Rome remains a very relative idea, for it rather leaves room for the possibility of an eternally repeatable renewal. Only in the Persian systems of mazdaism and zervanism can a clear distinction be perceived between a current, indefinite period of progressive decline—sometimes divided into four seasons, reminding one of Daniel 2 —and a definitive period, which is introduced by a general holocaust and a divine judgement. It is even not impossible that God may have used the influence of such Persian views in the building of his revela-

[1] Our principal source was: Mircea Eliade, *The Myth of the Eternal Return*, London, 1954.

tion concerning history within the Jewish people. It is generally felt that it is there that the meaning and consequences of the definitive and unrepeatable character of history were first made generally manifest.

This does not mean that the ancient experience of imitation, repetition and cyclic course of events is absent in Israel. It is no more absent there than it is in the great epoch-making peoples, and in fact we find clear traces of it in the Old Testament. A tendency to trace all current reality back to archetypal facts is firmly present not only in rabbinic literature, but also in the canonical books Exodus, Leviticus, Numbers, Deuteronomy and Joshua. Here all laws, social as well as religious, are retraced to incidents in the exodus, the wandering in the desert and the entry into the promised land, or at least to revelations which God gave to Moses. The most typical example of this sort of guarantee of primeval facts is to be seen in the law concerning the sabbath, which was not only given by Yahweh through his causing manna not to fall on the sabbath (Ex 16), but also finds exemplification in God's own day of rest after the work of creation (Gen 2 : 2ff.). For this reason the actual activity of creation is represented as having taken place during the first six days of a week (Gen 1).

In addition, it may already have been noted that Israel's institutions go back not so much to cosmic facts as to Yahweh's historic deeds, mostly in connection with the exodus. In Israel's feasts also, the celebration of these facts of salvation has assimilated and covered over the celebration of the seasons. The Jewish paschal feast, for example, still has the character of a feast of the first lambs and of one of the first harvest (the unleavened bread), but all this is explained entirely as a remembrance of the journey

33

out of Egypt, especially in the story of its institution (Ex 12; see also Deut 16: 3). These feasts are almost exclusively the celebration of a past. Only in the paschal meal of the new law is the Lord's death proclaimed 'until he comes' (1 Cor 11: 26). The idea of a 'golden era', then, is in no sense absent from Israel's religious experience. The golden period of the whole of humanity is the earthly paradise (Gen 2) which, however, is lost—in contrast to the myths of so many other peoples with noticeably more developed cultures—not by fate or a displeasure of the gods, but through a clear fault of man (Gen 3). And we also find traces of the idea of a general decline within human history: for example, in the long lives of those living before the flood (Gen 5) and Yahweh's decision to shorten them (Gen 6: 3), as also in the four kingdoms progressively declining in power described in Daniel 2, to which we have already referred above. Above all, however, God's people itself has its golden past, the representation of which becomes more and more grandiose as one gets further from it. This past consists chiefly of the period in the desert and the kingdom of David and Solomon. The prophets repeatedly call upon the deeds of God in the desert period in order to make the people more keenly aware of its obligations towards Yahweh, and the former existence with land, city and temple is the dream of the people during its exile. It is, however, mainly the desert period, and even more so the theocracy during the time of David and Solomon that appear in prophecies in the strict sense, in the predictions of the messianic future, of the reparation which God will achieve after Israel's purification. Here, then, we have apparently arrived at the summit of cyclic thought in Israel, so that we might be inclined to say that its conception of time and history does not differ essentially from the ahistorical and cyclic idea of time of the other peoples, both prehistorical and historical.

So far, however, the most important point has not been mentioned. For the most important element in Israel's conception of history is that it is completely oriented towards the 'day of Yahweh', and this makes it essentially different from the cyclic vision, in spite of all subordinate points of agreement. The very term 'day of Yahweh' indicates a unique ultimate time when word—and deed—will no longer be man's but those of the holy, most high God of Israel, as is clear from the overwhelming natural phenomena which are to accompany his appearance. Thus the essential difference between Israel's conception of history and the cyclic one lies in the element that we have already pointed out in the Persian system, namely the fact that the phase which is ushered in by this day is definitive, irreversible and irrevocable; purely and simply an end, an ultimate.

Before the exile this is not straightforwardly clear, for the intervention by Yahweh within the course of history itself, his divine judgements against Israel and the gentiles before the messianic reparation, are also referred to as his day. This definitive character becomes very clear, however, after the exile, when the last phase is situated in an 'other life', in a supermundane, heavenly sphere. This is done with most emphasis in the book of Daniel, where after the four kingdoms there will also be an eternal and heavenly kingdom founded by God. Thus, for example, in Dan 2:44: 'And in the days of those kings the God of heaven will set up a kingdom which shall never be destroyed, nor shall its sovereignty be left to another people. It shall break in pieces all these kingdoms and bring them to an end, and it shall stand for ever.' So also in the vision of the son of man who appears in the divine sphere 'with the clouds of heaven' (Dan 7: 13), and who receives universal dominion which is at the same time definitive: 'His dominion is an everlasting dominion, which shall not pass away' (Dan 7: 14). 'But the saints of the Most High shall receive the kingdom, and possess the kingdom for ever, and for ever and ever' (Dan 7: 18). 'Their kingdom shall be an everlasting kingdom, and all dominions shall serve and obey them' (Dan 7: 27). The unearthly, heavenly character of this eternal kingdom is still more accentuated by the fact that in the same prophecy of Daniel this consummation appears as achieved not just for a future generation of people dwelling on earth, but also for the dead, who will rise again: 'And many of those who sleep in the dust of the earth shall awake, some to everlasting life, and some to shame and everlasting contempt' (Dan 12: 2).

Here the idea of resurrection is new, and peculiar to Daniel and the time of the Macchabees (cf 2 Macch 7). However, the idea of the judgement which is contained in this, and treated at length in Wisdom 5, had long been prepared for by the prophets of Israel. For from Amos onward the day of Yahweh is not simply a day of blessing for Israel and of punishment for its enemies. For the sake of clarity, Amos completely reverses the expectations of his people: 'Why would you have the day of Yahweh? It is darkness, and not light' (Amos 5: 18), and then gives the reason for this, again in his paradoxical fashion, by saying that Yahweh loathes Israel's sacrifices, for he wants only justice and righteousness (Amos 5: 21–24). The prophets will continue to follow this line in preaching Israel's responsibility, as we saw in the previous section, when we spoke of their distinction between purely ritual holiness and personal holiness. During the time of exile Ezekiel will draw attention to personal responsibility and thereby to the personal justification or retribution of each separate individual (Ezek 18). Thus we have the preparation of what we just saw in Daniel and in the book of Wisdom, that the day of Yahweh brings with it a judgement on each individual's personal life. This means, then, that it is not only the beginning of a definitive phase after the history of this world, but also a judgement on that history and the harvest not only of what Israel and the nations, but also each person has sown during it. And in this way Israel clearly recognised history and its irrevocable decisions, not primarily in interhuman relations, but in relation to God and eternity. The blessing of Yahweh's day can be drawn from the model of earlier periods, but with its aspect of eternal judgement it surpassses them all. It is neither paradise nor the journey in the desert, nor the davidic kingdom, that is the ruling factor in Israel's conception of history, but this day of Yahweh. And so it may be said that Israel's vision of time and history is not cyclic, but linear; not repetitive, but eschatological.

If this is true of the people of the old revelation, then it comes out much more clearly when revelation is completed in the New Testament. There the Old Testament image of the eschaton is in the first place confirmed and unified. It is confirmed in as much as Jesus expressly defends the Old Testament teaching on the resurrection against the Sadducees (Mt 22:23–33); Mk 12:18–27; Lk 20:27–40), but above all through the fact that he himself rises from the dead as 'the first fruits of those who have fallen asleep' (1 Cor 15:20). In opposition to Greek thought, it is preached with emphasis that this is also a resurrection of the body, to the fullest extent by Saint Paul in 1 Cor 15, where at the same time the general resurrection is attributed to Christ's influence (vv.

37

21–23). In similar manner, the Old Testament teaching on the judgement is also confirmed in that it now appears that every person will be judged by the Christ, and this on their basic attitude towards God, even towards Christ himself (cf above all Mt 25). Thus Jesus resolutely places the definitive terminal phase in the supernatural and moral sphere. However, in the person of Jesus, all the data from the Old Testament concerning the eschaton are united. One can certainly point out pericopes which mainly concern the raising and congregating of the chosen ones, and there are others which chiefly describe the judgement, but these two are also bound into a unity, as for example, in Mt 24 and 25, and perhaps most explicitly in Jesus' statement about himself: 'The hour is coming when all who are in the tombs will hear his voice and come forth, those who have done good, to the resurrection of life, and those who have done evil, to the resurrection of judgement' (Jn 5: 28, 29).

With this christian revelation concerning the eschaton we see the linear and eschatological view of time and history completed. It should also be noticed in passing that by this the Old Testament image of history is not only completed, but also extended in a very basic way. For in the Old Testament everything was striving towards a future terminal point and in this the past served, as such, for making statements about the future, but is hardly, if at all, present as continuing reality. Thus, for example, after the Babylonian capivity Jerusalem and the temple are rebuilt, but the sceptre remains withheld from Judah. In the New Testament, on the other hand, the Christ who is to come has already come, yes, he has already risen and is present and active in the spirit as the first fruits of those who have fallen asleep. He is already 'the resurrection and the life'

(Jn 11 : 25). On the line of time the midpoint has become equally dominant with the endpoint, and the eschaton is today: for 'upon us the end of the ages has come' (1 Cor 10 : 11).

This reveals clearly how God makes history with man, and why not only at the end, but also in the course of the history of the world there are to be found 'days', 'hours' and 'seasons' of God. It is, then, not surprising that these words should appear so often in holy scripture: firstly 'the day of Yahweh' in the Old and 'the day of Christ' in the New Testament, but further also, Christ's 'hour' and the times and seasons fixed by the Father (Acts 1 : 7), and finally, the 'last days' and the 'last hour' (1 Jn 2 : 18). These words all indicate the way in which the God of the covenant is also a God of history.

We have now given a general indication of the way in which God's revelation in Israel and in Christ not only shows us his own historical activity with man, but also thereby brings man himself to that recognition and acceptance of his own history which is hardly found outside that revelation. The first task we set ourselves in this section is now completed, except that there remain two short remarks which must be made in order to avoid misunderstanding. The first is in connection with the way in which history is presented in the sources of revelation, the second with the relation between the history of God and man on the one hand, and human history on the other.

What we have to say about the sources of revelation is true mainly of holy scripture; it really only applies to tradition in so far as this takes over the biblical manner of speech and representation. Because scripture presents a history, it does not therefore mean that it is everywhere 'historical' in the

39

modern sense of that word. If by 'historical' we mean that it subjects its sources to a critical analysis and comparison, then in this sense no part of it may be described as historical. If we mean that it communicates facts which are in principle historically verifiable, then certainly not all of its statements are to be considered as historical. This is clearly true not only of all that scripture predicts in the way of future events, thus particularly regarding the eschaton, but it also holds in an ever-increasing measure as it goes further back into the primeval history of Israel and, above all, into that of the human race as a whole. For the story of paradise offers us facts which cannot be traced back along a chain of witnesses by us or by its writer. But it is not only the beginning and end of the biblical history of salvation that cannot be thus historically checked; there are also many facts in between which can only be negatively or indirectly verified, such as, for example, the virgin birth and Jesus' messianic identity and divinity. This distinction regarding historical verifiability was not, however, consciously recognised by the writers of the sacred books, so that it is necessary, particularly in the case of the 'biblical history of the beginning', that in retrospect we moderns dissociate the teaching from the apparently historical information that is only its clothing.

Thus the predicate 'historical', in the sense of 'historically verified' or 'historically verifiable in principle', may not, or at most only partly, be applied to the content of holy scripture. But in spite of all this it remains true that the bible is historical in a much more general and obvious sense, namely in as much as it communicates *facts,* facts which have been accomplished by God and man, decisive facts which have as their consequence a situation within this world or in the other life. Such a fact is the incarnation of God's Son, such a fact is his resurrection, his coming at the end of time and also man's fall at the beginning of his history, however much these two last facts may be affirmed by scripture in a prediction or a story whose elements can be described as mythical. Therefore the encyclical *Humani generis* points out 'that although the first eleven chapters of Genesis do not realise the principles of historical writing in the strict sense, such as the foremost Greek and Roman historians or the scholars of our own time have employed, they are nevertheless to be classed under the literary form of "historical writing" in a true sense, which should be investigated and more closely defined by exegetes' (n. 38).

We hope, then, to have indicated sufficiently that the history of salvation presented by scripture and tradition does really consist of facts. The question now, however, is: what facts? Apart from the 'history of the beginning' and the 'history of the end', the biblical history of salvation contains facts which almost exclusively take place within Israel, including the life of our Lord; it is only the church history described in the Acts of the Apostles that forms a sort of transition into a history that encompasses the world. However, should not the whole of human history since Christ, and perhaps also that before him, be included in the history of God and man? Or is there a reason for distinguishing the 'salvation history' presented by the bible from a 'profane history'? Let us begin our discussion of this point by noticing that in the salvation history of scripture facts are described which are decisive for the whole of humanity and which bring about a situation that cannot be avoided by anyone. From the history of the beginning there results the situation of original sin; from the whole of the Old Testament and the history of Christ there results the situation of revelation and of objective redemption; from the history of the last things, in so far as it renders the final judgement present, there results the eternal situation of salvation or rejection. The first two situations are decisive for every other history, but the facts of the remaining history do not themselves have a decisive character of such universality and influence upon the definitive fate of every human being. There thus seems to us to be every reason for preserving the traditional distinction between 'history of salvation' and 'profane history'.

But one must indeed see this as a distinction, and not make a radical separation out of it. For, on the one hand, the preparation of our salvation in the Old Testament is partly influenced by a whole profane history taking place round about it, which is why the king of Assyria is called Yahweh's razor, and Nebuchadnezzar and Cyrus his servants. And, as we shall presently explain in more detail, the Old Testament belongs to the history of salvation precisely because not only is its consummation in Christ, but it is itself of current and lasting importance to us. On the other hand, the proclamation of revelation and the application of objective redemption by the church create situations in which those that result from the history of salvation are more clearly demonstrated and realised. For this reason church history has a very special value as the meeting point of salvation history and profane history, as realisation of the instruction of the glorified Christ before his ascension and as the lasting epiphany of the Holy Spirit. The distinction between the history of salvation and profane history remains clearly visible, however, without injury to this mutual orientation. Therefore we should like to sum up what we have so far said in this section as follows: by his revelation and his creation of salvation history at the same time, God educates us to that idea of history which is accessible to our natural reason: he enters our history by making salvation history; in the history of salvation he shows himself to be a God of history.

God as the God of history

Having established this, we should like, in the remainder of this section, to investigate what this implies for God himself. This investigation can be brief, for we need alter nothing in the image of God that we drew in the previous section, regarding either the aspect of his transcendence or that of his covenant. God is transcendent with respect to the world, under all aspects, and thus independent of both the cyclic course of nature and the progress of history. The transcendence of God above time is his eternity. We can define that eternity of God philosophically by means of a comparison with time in which we eliminate all elements of imperfection. We then conclude that God's eternity is not only without beginning or end, but also without the change, the succession through which the fullness of our life is only ever experienced in part. And so we arrive at the classic definition of Boethius: 'interminabilis vitae tota simul et perfecta possessio', the perfect and all-inclusive possession of a life without beginning or end. Scripture, in contrast, limits itself to the negation of a beginning and end in God's existence. It finds God at the beginning and end of human history (Is 41: 1; 43: 12), as the one 'who was and is and is to come' (Rev 4: 8), and says to him: 'Of old thou didst lay the foundation of the earth, and the heavens are the work of thy hands. They will perish, but thou dost endure; but thou art the same, and thy years have no end' (Ps 102 (101): 25–27). The duration of God's life is therefore not rendered by an abstract concept of 'eternity', but by the joining together of an immense row of aeons, centuries, usually expressed by the well-known hebrew expression 'for ever and ever' ('in saecula saeculorum'). This biblical conception of eternity is thus related to the previously sketched biblical idea of time and history, and is therefore also currently referred to as a 'linear conception of eternity'. This description marks out in its users an opposition to the conception of eternity arising from Greek thought which is expressed in Boethius' definition. The awareness of this contrast may be of value in our reflection upon the faith, but it seems to us useless and also wrong to represent this opposition as irreconcilable. Let us therefore briefly show how both these definitions of God's eternity complement each other; thus what we said in the previous section about the divine image of the bible and that of reason finds its application here.

In the first place, it is certain that the biblical idea of God's eternity leaves room for more detailed reflection, such as that of Boethius. Scripture goes no further—explicitly, at least—than the denial of any beginning or end to the duration of God's existence, but this does not prevent us from going further and denying in God's existence the succession, the division of existence that is a basic quality of our temporality, and thus also any 'duration' in the strict sense of the word. We take this negative way in order to indicate the positive and infinite plenitude of God's life. For though scripture speaks about an activity of God which precedes or succeeds human activity, about divine predestination and providence, likewise about God's retribution and even about changes therein after human conversion, this seems to us no more of an objection against Boethius' conception of eternity than scriptural refer-

44

ences to God's face and hands are an objection against describing him as spirit in the fullest sense, or reference to God's wrath and repentance are a reason for denying his perfect happiness. The 'before' and 'after' in God's activity belong, just as much as his face, hands, wrath and repentance, to the descriptive, anthropomorphic terminology in which we talk about him. Scholastic theology may thus rest assured with respect to its use of the Boethian concept of eternity, at least in so far as it applies it to God. One might even wish that it had been more logically consistent in this application. In that case, in the ill-famed disputations at the end of the sixteenth and beginning of the seventeenth centuries concerning actual grace and free voluntary acts, it would not have conceived of the 'before' and 'after' in God's activity so literally as to ascribe a different structure to human freedom according to whether God's grace 'precedes' or 'only accompanies' it. It therefore seems to us a healthy consequence of the Boethian idea of divine eternity that the very problem underlying these disputations should be denied existence.

On the other hand, this cannot mean that what we have just referred to as the descriptive, anthropomorphic language of scripture should be set aside as worthless. As in the previous section, it must here be emphasised that this mode of speech is no poetic extra, but that it is necessary in addition to the language of philosophically purified concepts, indeed that these anthropomorphisms constitute the pre-eminent mode of speaking about God in scripture and to a great extent in tradition, precisely for the reason that they are necessary in order to reveal God's supernatural activity to us. In the previous section we developed this point with reference to God's covenant and his dialectical activity; let us now consider it with respect to the realisation of that covenant in history. As we have already said, God wishes to be not only stage-manager and producer of the human drama, but also a player in it, and in doing the latter he reveals an even greater perfection than in the first two roles. He is without relativity, yet related to man, and this not at some supertemporal moment of the latter's existence, but in the course of his history. Now this is expressed by representing God's activity as preceding or succeeding human activity, the former case being an image of his initiative, the latter of his reply, his re-action. For God's providence, particularly where it leads the chosen to salvation as predestination, precedes free human activity in the measure that it causes it, without, however, in any way eliminating its freedom (whence the danger in the term 'pre*determination*'), but rather by realising man's free decision both as a decision and as being free (which we shall try to illuminate in our next chapter with the aid of the doctrine on creation). But on the other hand, the carrying out of God's providential government of the world and of his predestination of the chosen is at the same time also reward or rejection, the answer to man's turning towards or away from God or of his conversion to him.

Here we may especially emphasise that God's providential care is *also* (not exclusively) an answer to man's search for the kingdom and justice of God; this theme has been treated a number of times by Romano Guardini. This author very rightly points out that although Jesus' promises must precede our efforts, they are still conditioned by our concern with the kingdom of God. For when Jesus warns us not to have any anxieties, and this with an a fortiori argument to the effect that the heavenly Father has given life and body, and that he also feeds the birds and clothes the lilies of the field (Mt 6: 25–31), then he ends by characterising this worry he has condemned as follows: 'For the gentiles seek all these things' (Mt 6: 32a), and follows this with the contrast: 'But seek first his (God's) kingdom and his righteousness, and all these things shall be yours as well' (Mt 6: 33). So what Jesus forbids is the solicitude of the heathen and what he orders is the seeking of the kingdom of God. It is only to this that the gift of 'all these things', of food and clothing, is joined. Thus, before any decision of ours the Father's providence already gives body and life, to animal and plant and still more so to man, to every man: 'for he makes his sun rise on the evil and on the good, and sends rain on the just and on the unjust' (Mt 5: 45). But it is only those who seek his kingdom and righteousness whom he provides lastingly with food and clothing and 'all these things'. It thus appears here that divine providence, which we tend to think of as depending purely on God's initiative, is at the same time an answer to the human being's conversion to the kingdom of God. In this way, then, God's activity is a dialogue with man in the course of his history.

We hope hereby to have given an adequate treatment of the second and final point of this second section. We should now like to conclude this section and the whole of this first chapter by bringing together the themes we have considered in the first article of faith, which forms the title of this chapter: 'God, the Father almighty.' As is clear from the headings and whole content of our two sections, we have given more attention to 'God' than we have to 'Father'. And we should still like to reserve discussion of the more important aspects of God's fatherhood until we can consider him through his Son, who gives us 'power to become children of God' (Jn 1:

47

12). However, basing ourselves on the content which we have attributed, mainly from the Old Testament, to the notions of 'God of the covenant' and 'God of history', we may now say something further about the 'Father almighty'.

First, his omnipotence. It is not certain whether the expression *El shaddai* may be accurately translated in the stories of the patriarch as 'the almighty God'—some think that the name includes a reference to fertility. It is without doubt, however, that in the prophets and the literature of wisdom (it appears most of all in the Book of Job) it expresses God's omnipotence. Yahweh is almighty or all-dominating particularly in his rule over the fortunes of his people and of the nations. It is the same with God's eternity, as when in Deutero-Isaiah we find this irresistible power of his contrasted against the forces which are oppressing God's people. The nations are nothing to Yahweh (Is 40: 17); nor are their gods (41: 1–7); even nature cannot resist him (43: 11–21); his word accomplishes all that he has sent it to do (52: 11). The connection between this omnipotence of God and his eternity, which is here continually presupposed, becomes clear in the formula in Revelation 1: 8 which thus sums up Christ: 'I am the Alpha and the Omega, says the Lord God, who is and who was and who is to come, the Almighty.' It is clear that this omnipotence is not only directed against gentiles and sinners, but also and in the first place works on behalf of the people of God. Thus it is, together with all God's faithfulness and love and eternity, a reason for confidence, for hope. Even if in Genesis *El shaddai* does not yet mean 'God almighty', then for Abraham the comprehensive formulation of his faith is still that which Yahweh spoke in reply to Sarah's laughter: 'Is anything too hard for Yahweh?' (Gen 18: 14), which God's

48

angel will repeat to Mary at the dawning of the new covenant (Lk 1: 37).

This almighty God is not only God of the covenant, but also Father; not only 'our God', but also 'our God and Father'. In the Old Testament, this covenant relationship between Yahweh and Israel is most directly expressed by the image of marriage, which we discussed in the preceding section. Yahweh is also 'Father' by reason of the tenderness of this relationship between him and Israel (Hos 11: 1–4; Jer 3: 4, 19; Prov 3: 12; Heb 12: 6–8). But Israel's privilege of 'sonship' or 'adoption' (Rom 9: 4) goes back in the first place to the fact that Yahweh chose it out, even made and reared it in the liberation from Egypt (Deut 32: 6; Is 1: 2; 64: 8). But Israel also continues to call Yahweh 'Father' because of his lasting care (Is 63: 16). This relationship holds especially between Yahweh and the kings of the davidic dynasty (2 Sam 7: 14; Ps 2: 7; 89 (88): 27ff.; 110 (109): 37), and is only completely fulfilled in the son of David, who is pre-eminently the annointed one and son of God. However, it is not only this activity, through which Yahweh builds up his people and royal line in history, that is a reason for calling him a Father; he is also a Father to the just at the last judgement (Wisdom 5: 5). To the latter is joined the New Testament revelation of God's fatherhood, for this begins with the exhortation to 'become' sons of God (Mt 5: 45) and goes on to make clear that we are only capable of this in Christ (Jn 1: 12), that through him we shall not only be such in eternity, but that we are already so (1 Jn 3: 1ff.). As we have already indicated, we are not going to discuss here the depths of Christ's own sonship and of ours in him. Thus at present we shall merely point out that, like Christ's redemption, this fatherhood of God in the New Testament is meant for all mankind and that even now the Father cares for all those who seek his kingdom on earth. In this connection we would refer to the quotations we gave above concerning the Father's providence. Let us end here with a word on the Father's universal desire to care for and save us: 'So it is not the will of your Father who is in heaven that one of these little ones should perish' (Mt 18: 14); and: 'Again, I say to you, if two of you agree on earth about anything they ask, it will be done for them by my Father in heaven' (Mt 18: 19). It is to this God that Jesus teaches us to pray in the 'Our Father' (Mt 6: 9–13; Lk 11: 2–4). And the whole of this consoling teaching must be before us whenever we profess: 'I believe in God, the Father almighty.'

2

'The creator of heaven and earth'

In the beginning God created the heavens and the earth. The earth was without form and void, and darkness was upon the face of the deep; and the Spirit of God was moving over the face of the waters.

And God said, 'Let there be light'; and there was light. And God saw that the light was good; and God separated the light from the darkness. God called the light Day and the darkness he called Night. And there was evening and there was morning, one day.

And God said, 'Let there be a firmament in the midst of the waters, and let it separate the waters from the waters.' And God made the firmament and separated the waters which were under the firmament from the waters which were above the firmament. And it was so. And God called the firmament Heaven. And there was evening and there was morning, a second day.

And God said, 'Let the waters under the heavens be gathered together in one place, and let the dry land appear.' And it was so. God called the dry land Earth, and the waters that were gathered together he called Seas. And God saw that it was good. And God said, 'Let the earth put forth vegetation, plants yielding seed, and fruit trees bearing fruit in which is their seed, each according to its kind, upon the earth.' And it was so. The earth brought forth vegetation, plants yielding seed according to their own kinds, and trees bearing fruit in which is their seed, each according to its kind. And God saw that it was good. And there was evening and there was morning, a third day.

And God said, 'Let there be lights in the firmament of the heavens to separate the day from the night; and let them be for signs and for seasons and for days and years, and let them be lights in the firmament of the heavens to give light upon the earth.' And it was so. And God made the two great lights, the greater light to rule the day, and the lesser light to rule the night; he made the stars also. And God set them in the firmament of the heavens to give light upon the earth, to rule over the day and over the night, and to separate the light from the darkness. And God saw that it was good. And there was evening and there was morning, a fourth day.

And God said, 'Let the waters bring forth swarms of living creatures, and let birds fly above the earth across the firmament of the heavens.' So God created the great sea monsters and every living creature that moves, with which the waters swarm, according to their kinds, and every winged bird according to its kind. And God saw that it was good. And God blessed them, saying, 'Be fruitful and multiply and fill the waters in the seas, and let birds multiply on the earth.' And there was evening and there was morning, a fifth day.

And God said, 'Let the earth bring forth living

creatures according to their kinds: cattle and creeping things and beasts of the earth according to their kinds.' And it was so. And God made the beasts of the earth according to their kinds and the cattle according to their kinds, and everything that creeps on the ground according to its kind. And God saw that it was good.

Then God said, 'Let us make man in our image, after our likeness; and let them have dominion over the fish of the sea, and over the birds of the air, and over the cattle, and over all the earth, and over every creeping thing that creeps upon the earth.' So God created man in his own image, in the image of God he created him; male and female he created them. And God blessed them, and God said to them, 'Be fruitful and multiply, and fill the earth and subdue it; and have dominion over the fish of the sea and over the birds of the air, and over every living thing that moves upon the earth.' And God said, 'Behold, I have given you every plant yielding seed which is upon the face of all the earth, and every tree with seed in its fruit; you shall have them for food. And to every beast of the earth, and to every bird of the air, and to everything that creeps upon the earth, everything that has the breath of life, I have given every green plant for food.' And it was so. And God saw everything that he had made, and behold, it was very good. And there was evening and there was morning, a sixth day.

Thus the heavens and the earth were finished, and all the host of them. And on the seventh day God finished his work which he had done, and he rested on the seventh day from all his work which he had done. So God blessed the seventh day and hallowed it, because on it God rested from all his work which he had done in creation.

These are the generations of the heavens and
the earth when they were created.

Genesis 1 : 1–2 : 4a

From our introduction and first chapter it will have
become sufficiently clear that in these dialogues we
are revealing the content of our faith by returning to
its sources, and that in doing so it is only in passing
that we are speaking about what the natural reason
can discover unaided. This is also indicated by the
order of our first two chapters. If it had been our
intention first to hear from our reason and then to
establish what revelation has to add, then we should
have considered God firstly as creator of heaven and
earth, and only after that as God of covenant and
salvation history and as the almighty Father. In
doing that we should have been following not only
an apologetical plan, but also that of the present
edition of the bible, and in particular that of the
book of Genesis, although the latter in no sense presents its account of creation as the fruit of human
speculation. Thus one must certainly not condemn
those who would wish to speak of God firstly as
creator and secondly as father, not only for apologetical motives, but also in order to reveal in a
better way the particular nature of God's fatherhood. If, on the other hand, one wishes to retrace
the development of divine faith in Israel and in
christianity, then the required order is the one given
by the first article of the Apostles' Creed. In order to
thus approach the sources as much as possible in
their concrete situation we shall deal with the account of creation in this second chapter, having
steeped ourselves in the biblical notion of God in
the first, whilst in the third we shall cover the same
ground, but in the opposite direction. In its turn,
this second chapter will be divided into two sections,

of which the first will present what the sources have to say, and the second a more systematic treatment of the idea of creation. What we said of the previous chapter holds also for this one: it gives, on the one hand, more than natural reason can discover, even as regards the same subject, but on the other it does not intend to exhaust the riches of revelation concerning this subject, for, like the complete notion of God, the view of creation must be completed in the acknowledgement of Christ, the redemption, the Holy Spirit and the ultimate consummation.

1 *The doctrine of creation from its sources*

As we have already indicated above, we consider the truth that God is the creator of the world, like the existence of God, to be accessible to the natural reason of man. This theoretical capability of knowledge concerning the creation has not been affirmed by the church as dogma in the way that natural knowledge of God's existence has. If, in its definition concerning the natural capacity to know God, the First Vatican Council calls him: 'God, the principle and goal of all things' (Dz 1785) or 'the one true God, our creator and lord' (Dz 1806), then these additional clarifications do not oblige us to accept as a point of faith that God is also knowable to our natural reason as principle and goal, as creator and lord. But, although this natural possibility of knowledge of the creation is thus not an explicitly asserted point of faith, it is nevertheless obvious. For if it is in principle possible for our natural reason to progress from the world to God, it seems to us to require only a further reflection upon this first process of knowledge in order to see God also as origin and explanation, not only of those finite things which made his existence knowable to us, but also of all finite things and persons, of the whole world, and

55

that as a perfectly transcendental origin and as a completely free cause, in other words, as creator. We therefore believe that the truth that God is creator falls among 'ea quae in rebus divinis humanae rationi per se impervia non sunt', as the First Vatican Council puts it (Dz 1786), those divine matters which in themselves are not inaccessible to our reason.

However, when the same council says, concerning these divine truths, that a universal, easily attainable, certain and undisturbed knowledge of them must be attributed to divine revelation (ibid.), then this must be said to be even more true of creation than of the existence of God as such. The encyclical *Humani generis* goes still further into detail in an explanation which is particularly applicable to the teaching on creation. 'For matters concerning God and the relations between God and men,' it says, 'are truths which surpass the order of sensory perception and which, when they are applied in practical life and give it its full realisation, require personal commitment and self-denial. The human mind, however, when it wishes to make such truths its own, experiences difficulties through the pressure of senses and imagination, as also through the uncontrolled tendencies which are the consequence of original sin. And thus it comes about that in such circumstances people readily deceive themselves into thinking false or at least doubtful that which they in fact do not wish to be true.' The truth that God is creator requires a very radical correction of our representations, for senses and imagination bring us only into contact with human making and producing, and this is always a making out of something that already exists. In addition, this truth implies the basic limitation and complete dependence of created reality. This is opposed by the 'pride of life' (1 Jn 2:16), which tries to flee into one of the many forms of magical pantheism or undemanding deism. And in fact, outside of judaeo-christian revelation there is little, if any, pure doctrine of creation to be found. Just as with respect to the recognition of history, here also the situation of primitive man is in principle the same as that of men from the civilised peoples. Everywhere, either in mythical cosmogonies or in philosophical speculations concerning the origin of the world, we see the result of the natural human capacity to know the creation and of the opposing forces which we indicated. On the one hand, the origin of the world is connected with God or gods and presented in a primitive or philosophical manner as something unique and sublime. On the other, the notion of human fabrication continues to override the whole of this doctrine, either in the mythical form of conflict against an archetypal serpent, a chaos without origin, or in the philosophical idea of a pre-existent matter or world of ideas, or perhaps in the form of a necessarily occurring emanation, or again in that of a totally absent godhead that leaves creation and the maintenance of what has been created to demiurges. Such is the situation in which the revelation of God's creation came to the world through Israel, in which it was confronted primarily with primitive, mythological cosmogonies. Here again we must begin in Ur of the Chaldees.

The doctrine of God's creation did not come into the midst of these human speculations as a completed formulation falling from heaven. It is in the first place contained in the all-dominating and supremely eloquent fact of Abraham's and Israel's meeting with the living God. The latter shows himself as Yahweh, the God of Israel, but also as God purely and simply, the only God of all the world. And in Israel's history the gods and also the natural reality of Egypt, the heart and the military forces of

Pharaoh, the peoples of Canaan and the land of the two rivers, in brief, the whole of nature and history, appear as subject to Yahweh's authority. He rules all of it, he holds it in his hands, and this naturally leads to the realisation that he is the maker of everything, even of man himself.

It is quite possible that in the achievement of this last step a helping influence may have been exercised by the ancient cosmogonic myths which Israel had received from its semitic surroundings. But it is still true that Israel's monotheism completely transformed them into expressions of an authentic doctrine of creation. Thus revelation does not first engender faith in God the creator and thence faith in the God of Israel, but the other way round. The first chapter of Genesis is certainly one of the most recent parts of the whole book; it is even a product, though an early one, of the latest of the great forms of Old Testament literature, namely wisdom literature. This opening chapter of the present edition of the bible may therefore be regarded as a summary of various passages in which Israel's faith in the creation is rather more incidentally, though no less clearly, confessed, passages which may perhaps be contemporary with Genesis 1, or later than it, but some of which could have preceded it. We shall not, however, stop here to date those Old Testament passages which concern creation. For this reason we shall not further add to this short introduction by indicating the traces of the belief in creation prior to its crystallisation in Genesis 1, but proceed immediately with the treatment of this chapter. In doing so we hope to provide an example of the spirit in which we wish at all times to read holy scripture; a spirit which, in order to make the religious essence more manifest, does not allow itself to be hindered by incidentals. Following this exegesis of Genesis 1

58

we shall further clarify the religious value of the doctrine of creation by running through the most important passages in which the Old Testament expresses its faith in the creation. Finally, we should also like to point out more or less the same elements of a creation doctrine in the church of the New Testament.

Genesis 1

More strictly speaking, the creation story with which our present book of Genesis opens and from which it principally derives its name runs from 1 : 1 to 2 : 3 (probably even to 2 : 4a) inclusive.[1] For the beginning of chapter 2, which is concerned with God's sabbath-day rest, is an essential element, if not of the doctrine of creation itself, then certainly of that which this pericope intends to present. By speaking about essential elements and incidentals we are indicating a distinction and even the possibility of a certain dissociation between the two. God speaks at all times, and always has those he sends speak, in a certain situation, to a certain human community, at a certain point of human history. This is also true of the preaching of the apostles and of Jesus himself, and it remains true of what the church is saying in our days. We recognise this very clearly in the Old Testament, however, particularly in those modes of presentation which we experience today as 'primitive'. To these belongs the world-view of Genesis 1 and of the whole bible. The earth was thought of as a disc in the midst of the seas, fixed upon columns coming out of the bottomless depths, and above it the heavenly dome, which could let the rain through.

[1] For what is said here about Genesis 1, we owe much to the series of articles 'Israels visie op het verleden' by H. Renckens sj, in vols 17 (1950)–20 (1953) of the catechetical periodical *Verbum*.

Now we believe that it is abundantly clear that this world-view does not belong to the direct content of the doctrine of creation, but is only a presupposition in terms of which this doctrine is presented. We may thus exclude this world-view from our further reflection, but not contemptuously, for it allows us to see how God addressed the human beings of that age and that people in the language of their thoughts and fantasy, how even in this connection he did not disdain to be their God.

When we now further consider how, proceeding from this world-view, the story of creation is described, we discover a certain order among what has been created and at the same time a certain duration of God's activity. These, also, belong in the first place to the terminology, but they also point to an element of the doctrine, although not to its main theme. First a few divisions are made in creation: in the first place that between light and darkness, next that between the waters above the firmament and the waters beneath it, and then that between the sea and the dry land with its vegetation. After this making of divisions, God fills the various spaces, namely the firmament of the heavens with stars, the sea with fish and water creatures, the air with birds and finally the earth with animals and with men. The relations here indicated among creatures certainly belong to the primitive world-view and not to the doctrinal content, except for one. This is the relation of man to the rest of creation, whereby 'in God's image and after his likeness' he has dominion over it (Gen 1 : 26ff.). It is with special emphasis that the writer narrates this creation of man and even suggests a certain paradisical situation of peace between man and beast (Gen 1 : 29), so that 'everything that God had made was very good' (Gen 1 : 31). This special creation and destination of man forms the

60

theme of Genesis 2 and of Psalm 8, and is spoken of in passing further on in the bible, which is why we also believe that it belongs to the doctrinal content. However, we shall not discuss this point here.

We shall also pass by the teaching which is connected with the hebdomadal plan followed by Genesis 1:1–2:3. Any concordism that claims to find there agreement with periods in the development of the universe must, we believe, be rejected as a view that has already been transcended. The meaning of this division into days of a week lies in God's sabbath-day rest (Gen 2:2) and in the divine obligation upon men, indicated by the words: 'God blessed the seventh day and hallowed it' (Gen 2:3). That the sabbath rest is an obligation by reason of the covenant with Yahweh is made clear in the decalogue, both in the reading of Exodus (20:8–11) and in that of Deuteronomy (5:12–15). The latter bases itself upon God's liberation of his people from slavery in Egypt, Exodus upon the week of creation, thus connecting with what we find in Genesis. There we see the procedure by which this divine decree is grounded in an exemplary deed of God (just as in Ex 16, in fact, where Yahweh only makes the manna rain down for six days), a procedure that gives evidence of the primitive mentality, as we have already seen in section 2 of our first chapter. However, the doctrine of the divine decree concerning the sabbath need not be discussed at this point, and we shall therefore immediately proceed to the main theme of Genesis 1: God creates everything.

Here we are using the word 'create' as a technical term for the christian and theological idea of this completely unique activity of God. The Old Testament does not yet possess such a technical term. Yet it is already in the process of development. The verb *bara* refers, in this verbal form, exclusively to a

61

making by God, and that a making which brings forth something completely new, something new that only God can bring forth. One thinks, for example, of the prayer in the Miserere: 'Create (Vulgate *crea*) in me a clean heart, O God, and put a new and steadfast spirit within me' (Ps 51 (50): 10). The completely renewing, completely 'creative' activity of God that is indicated by *bara* is sometimes his 're-creation' in the messianic future, but usually the bringing about of the great basic elements of nature: light and darkness, the heavenly bodies and the winds, mankind, the peoples. It is noteworthy that in Deutero-Isaiah, that majestic vision of history and the messianic re-creation from the standpoint of Yahweh's eternity and creative power (to be seen already in Is 40), *bara* appears quite often, and with the meaning of 'first creation' (Is 40: 26; 42: 5; 43: 1, 7; 45: 12, 18; 54: 16; see also Ezek 28: 13, 15; Mal 2: 10), although with at the same time a certain prospect of the re-creation. And thus *bara* starts to become a technical term. Now the writer of the first story of creation also makes use of this term for God's activity, through which equally 'the heavens and the earth' (Gen 1: 1), the beasts (Gen 1: 21), as also man (Gen 1: 27) come to be. So we may expect a priori, on account of the use of this verb, that we are going to be told about a very special form of productive activity. If we now go to the story itself and consider together the various aspects of this divine activity, then its completely unique character becomes even more clear. In order to reveal this unique deed of God, it appears that the story itself must be unique and, even though it may have its roots in ancient mythological cosmogonies from the semitic world, the fruit of a radical 're-creation'.

Indeed, this is seen as soon as we ask the question: who is creating here? It is God, called 'Elohim', but the same as Yahweh, the God of Israel, as is clear from the composition of the whole book of Genesis and in particular from chapters 2 and 3, which also under this aspect form a transition between the first account of creation and the rest of the book in that there God is constantly referred to by the double name 'Yahweh Elohim'. Now this God creates completely alone, and this monotheism radically distinguishes Genesis 1 from all the cosmogonies in which gods co-operate or oppose, or even come into existence, from the cosmogonies which are at the same time theogonies. In this story only God is active, and other gods do not appear. Even the words 'sun' and 'moon' are avoided by means of a paraphrase (Gen 1: 16), probably because in the semitic milieu they were also names of gods. Only once do we come up against a plural which is difficult to explain, namely when God says: 'Let *us* make man' (Gen 1: 16). The majestic plural is unusual in Hebrew, and a suggestion of the mystery of the Holy Trinity seems to us somewhat far-fetched. Perhaps the presence of angels at the creation is supposed, as in Job 38: 7. Then the plural would at the same time serve to emphasise that in the next verse the word *elohim*, which is a plural noun in any case, also has a plural meaning and is thus used as a generic noun, not as a proper name. It is there stated (Gen 1: 27b), concerning man: 'in (as) the image of God he created him', but this is not to be conceived of as 'the image of Yahweh personally', but as 'image of the divine world' (cf Ps 8: 6). Thus we do not need to think here of a terminological relic from a polytheistic source, and so the mode of speech does not lag behind the strictly monotheistic thought.

Such a discrepancy between thought and mode of expression does reveal itself, however, when one now asks the question: *out of what* does God create? We

63

are by now in the habit of giving the answer: out of nothing, an answer whose meaning we shall further investigate in the next section. The expression 'out of nothing' finds a biblical origin in the words of the Macchabees' mother: 'Consider the heavens and the earth, and all they contain; consider that God made all of this, and mankind too, out of nothing' (2 Macch 7: 28). But in Genesis 1 there is no such expression. In fact, as far as modes of speech are concerned, our story is closer to several passages in which God's creation is still represented in some measure as his victory over the chaos or the primeval sea, Rahab; thus in Psalm 89 (88): 10: 'Thou didst crush Rahab like a carcass.' For a chaotic situation of earth and sea exists at the beginning of Genesis 1, and of it verse 2 says: 'The earth was without form and void, and darkness was upon the face of the deep.' One may now say that even this chaos is a result of God's creation, for beforehand in verse 1 we find: 'In the beginning God created the heavens and the earth.' It seems a very likely possibility, however, that this first verse is not intended to represent an all-preceding archetypal deed, a *prima creatio*, of which the formless and void earth and the primeval world sea are the result, these being subsequently ordered in a 'second creation'; rather that verse 1 is simply an opening summary of the whole story, just as Genesis 2: 4a appears to be a closing summary. This view seems more in keeping with the parallelistic and concentric thought of the bible and with the traces of a chaos in other passages, which is why we must at least take it into consideration.

On this interpretation, then, the whole of the creation in Genesis 1 is in the first place an ordering and filling of what God encountered in the beginning as 'without form and void'. Even so, it is still striking that here the chaos itself nevertheless shows no activity or life whatsoever. It is no living being, no primeval serpent that is killed and divided up; in this story it is no longer even 'trodden upon like a carcass', it is not any sort of resistance. One could perhaps go further and say that this *tohuwabohu* of Genesis 1:2 is a concrete expression for the 'nothing' of our definitions. For by this 'nothing' we mean the complete opposite of that which is, of being. Now the writer of Genesis 1 intended to express the same thing. But in the bible 'being' means 'being present', which also includes the ordering and thus the usefulness of the world. It is precisely in opposition to this that the chaos stands. Being equals cosmos, thus chaos equals non-being. If this interpretation is correct, then Genesis 1 stands closer to a 'creation out of nothing' than the presence of a chaos would make one suspect. But even if this is not the case, God is still the only active agent.

Let us now put the question: *what* does God create? It appears that the result of this activity of God alone is the whole visible world. For God created 'the heavens and the earth' (Gen 1:1, 2:4a) or 'the heavens and the earth and the whole host of them' (Gen 2:1), i.e., 'the heavens and the earth with all that they contain' (2 Macch 7:28), 'the heavens and the earth with all that is admired beneath the heavens' (Ex 13:10). For a true oriental such as the writer of Genesis 1 it was not enough to express this by such summary formulae as the above; no, he must name everything and point it out, as it were, and thus we see him occupied in doing this according to the primitive conception which he had of the world and the classification which he introduced therein. Of importance in this regard are the words: 'each according to its kind' (Gen 1:21, 24) and 'everything that . . .' (Gen 1:21, 25), by which is indicated that not only the living beings mentioned, but also

65

everything that can be counted under the names enumerated is the creation of God. Thus the intention of the writer appears to be to present the whole of the visible cosmos as the result of God's creation. The invisible beings, the angels, are not mentioned here. These appear throughout scripture as courtiers, armed powers and servants of God, by which their dependence upon him is made clear. Only once are they classified among the creatures of God, namely in the song of the three young men (Dan 3:58). With this scripture also confessed God as 'creator of all things, visible and invisible'.

One last question remains in order for us to reveal more clearly the content of Genesis 1, namely: *how* or *through what* does God create? The answer to this will show us that, certainly as regards the representation of God's creative act, Genesis 1 constitutes a summit in Old Testament revelation. We human beings cannot think of this deed other than by proceeding from our human productive activity and purifying our concept of it. Primitive man did this by representing his creator-god as fighting against a living chaos or giving form to existing matter. Nor is such imagery foreign to the Old Testament. We have already referred to the fight against Rahab (Ps 89 (88):11) and for the formation of creatures, in particular of man by God's hands, we can point to the story of paradise and to various other passages (Gen 2:7, 19; Ps 8:4; Ps 19 (18):2; Ps 94 (93):9; Ps 95 (94):4ff.; Ps 102 (101):26; Ps 119 (118):73; Job 10:8–11). Especially this last representation has a deep religious value in that it gives the feeling that everything, above all man in all his physical nature, is of God. But the majesty of God's activity and its transcendence above all human activity is nevertheless most clearly expressed by the manner in which God creates, namely through his word. In Genesis 1

66

there is no talk of God's hands. There is perhaps one single suggestion of such imagery when it is said, concerning the heavenly bodies, that 'God *set* them in the firmament of the heavens' (Gen 1:17). The separation of the elements certainly does not need to be conceived of as a work of God's hands, since elsewhere in scripture the separation of sea and land is ascribed to Yahweh's command (Ps 33 (32):6–7; Ps 104 (103):7; Job 38:11—although on the other hand, Ps 89 (88):11). What is expressly said in Genesis 1 about God's creative act, however, is that he spoke: 'And God said, "Let there be light"; and there was light' (Gen 1:3). This is repeated literally or in an equivalent expression a further seven times in the same chapter (Gen 1:6, 9, 11, 14f., 20f.). This chapter may thus be considered as summed up by the ninth verse of Psalm 33 (32): 'For he spoke, and it came to be; he commanded, and it stood forth.' And also by an earlier sentence in the same psalm: 'By the word of Yahweh the heavens were made, and all their host by the breath of his mouth' (Ps 33 (32):6). For in Genesis 1 'the spirit of God was moving over the face of the waters' (Gen 1:2), before he spoke. This may also be translated: the breath of God (Bible de Jérusalem: 'le souffle d'Élohim'). Together with the chaos there is a promise in the form of God's breath, which is soon to bear the word that will bring forth all things. We said earlier that the definition 'creating is making out of nothing' cannot be read explicitly in Genesis 1. Now, on the contrary, we may establish that according to Genesis 1 creation is making solely through one's word, and this definition is just as sublime, and in fact more positive. We may safely say that precisely for this reason Genesis 1 constitutes the summit of Old Testament teaching on creation.

67

The rest of the old testament

By analysing Genesis 1 we have sufficiently clearly described this doctrine under the aspect which we should like to call its metaphysical content. It now remains for us to survey its religious significance. What are the feelings and attitudes towards God that it causes in man? Here we shall more or less leave the creation story of Genesis 1 in order to give a survey—which is in no way complete—of various Old Testament passages concerning God's creative act and power. These will come from the prophets and, more so, from the psalms. We shall be able to pick out first those texts in which the creation is considered more or less on its own, and then a somewhat greater number in which awareness of the creation accompanies that of the covenant.

Looking back at the breaking forth of faith in creation from the old cosmogonies and theogonies, one sees that it may be regarded as a liberation. The reflectively thought-out expression of this, however, is something that one cannot expect in ancient Israel, although we may perhaps be able to hear something of this liberation in Genesis 1 itself, in the often repeated and thereby so firmly emphasised words: 'And God saw that it was good' (Gen 1:4, 10, 12, 18, 21, 25), summed up after the creation of man thus: 'And God saw everything that he had made, and behold, it was very good' (Gen 1:31). This point is especially meaningful in the context of the whole book of Genesis. In coming from God, everything is good; evil comes from man's sin against God, in which scripture certainly sees present a permission and activity of God, but which on the other hand is expressly contrary to God's will and first plan, as we learn from Genesis 2 and 3.

From this thought of God's good creation the way

stands open for _admiration and praise._ This we find
above all in certain psalms. The most directly expressed of these is the long creation psalm, Ps 104
(103), which is simply one astonished cry of jubilation over Yahweh's majesty in his works. Shorter,
and concentrating above all on the place of man in
God's creation, Psalm 8 expresses the same thought,
as is clear from the opening and closing verse: 'O
Yahweh, our Lord, how majestic is your name in all
the earth!' (Ps 8:2, 10). The first half of Psalm
19 (18) also expresses this idea with a strong emphasis on the 'narration' and 'speaking' of creation,
or as we would say, on creation as 'natural revelation', for 'the heavens are telling the glory of God'
(Ps 19 (18): 1). This majesty is at the same time his
exaltedness, his holiness, as we have described in the
previous chapter. This is why Psalm 24 (23), a psalm
about Yahweh's sanctuary and his ark, begins with
the words: 'The earth is the Lord's and the fullness
thereof, the world and those who dwell therein; for
he has founded it upon the seas and established it
upon the rivers' (Ps 24 (23): 1), and goes on: 'Who
shall ascend the hill of Yahweh? And who shall
stand in his holy place? He who has clean hands and
a pure heart' (Ps 24 (23): 3, 4a). Still more clear is the
call in Isaiah 66: 1ff. upon God's deed of creation in
order to bring out the relativeness of the external
cult (cf Acts 7: 48–50) and to demand _inward holi-
ness_ (cf also Ps 50 (49): 8–15). But God's transcendence is discerned from his creative action in a much
fuller and more grandiose manner at the end of the
book of Job (38–42), as has also been mentioned in
our first chapter. Here it is God himself who, referring to his creation, says to the man Job: 'Who is
this that darkens counsel by words without knowledge?' (Job 38: 2). However, not only God's transcendence, but also _his uniqueness—or rather his_

existence compared with the non-existence of the idols—may be seen from creation. Jeremiah and Baruch speak in this sense. 'The gods who did not make the heavens and the earth shall perish from the earth and from under the heavens. It is Yahweh who made the earth by his power . . .' etc. (Jer 10 : 11–16). In the letter of Jeremiah the gods are estimated lower than the phenomena of nature, which must after all obey God (Baruch 6 : 59–62). The possibility of knowledge of the creator from his creation is a further reflection on this latter. This is referred to, once more in polemic against idolatry, by the author of the book of Wisdom, who is imitated in this regard by Saint Paul (Rm 1 : 19f.). As a conclusion to this reflection, which has more or less exclusively considered the creation, let us add the following passage from the book of Wisdom:

> For all men who were ignorant of God were foolish by nature; and they were unable from the good things that are seen to know him who exists, nor did they recognise the craftsmen while paying heed to his works; but they supposed that either fire or wind or swift air, or the circle of the stars, or turbulent water, or the luminaries of heaven were the gods that rule the world.
>
> If through delight in the beauty of these things men assumed them to be gods, let them know how much better than these is their Lord, for the author of beauty created them.
>
> And if men were amazed at their power and working, let them perceive from them how much more powerful is he who formed them.
>
> For from the greatness and beauty of created things comes a corresponding perception of their Creator [Wisdom 13 : 1–5].

In the quotations so far the main accent has been laid upon the creative act of God, but usually it has also already been clear that this creator is the God of Israel. How great, therefore, is Israel's God and how majestic the covenant with him! We have already heard this in Ps 8: 1: 'O Yahweh, our Lord, how majestic is your name in all the earth!' This realisation receives a special emphasis in the wisdom section of the prophecy of Baruch. God, the creator, it is there asserted, is our God; he has withheld wisdom from the other nations, but given it to Israel as his law (Baruch 3: 32–4: 1). The fact that Yahweh is the mighty creator of the heavens and the earth, however, is above all an infinite source of confidence for the weak Israel. This theme admits several variations. It appears in the Deutero-Isaiah (Is 40: 12, 26; 45: 18; 48: 13) as the basis of God's solicitude for Israel in his dominion over the world. The mother of the Macchabees, whose remark concerning creation 'out of nothing' we have already cited, thereby presents the grounds for hope in its highest form, the hope for resurrection (2 Macch 7: 27–29). But more usual is the hope for Israel's salvation through the creative power of God. This is expressed by the prayer of Mordecai: on account of Yahweh's creative power, no one can resist him if it is his will to save Israel (Esther 13: 9–11).

But in the psalms we find above all praise or supplication. Psalm 33 (32): 4–9, parts of which we have already quoted as a summary of Genesis 1, preaches confidence in Yahweh's almighty word, because by it he created. Psalm 89 (88), that insistent prayer for fulfilment of the promise which Yahweh had made in a former age to David and of which nothing seemed to have come, describes God's fight with the sea and with Rahab, and the creation of the world in all its extension (vv. 10–13), to then bless the fortune of the people that rejoices in Yahweh's name and receives his promises. Psalm 95 (94), the invitational psalm of the divine office, is again filled with the majesty of Israel's God, who is also the creator of all things (vv. 4f.), and therefore warns against defying him as did their fathers in the desert. In Psalm 102 (101), the prayer for return from exile, God's creative power and eternity are the reason for asking to stay in his sight. The ultimate depth of Israel's need, but also of Yahweh's salvation, is summarised in the short Psalm 124 (123), which ends with the confession which also appears separately in the christian liturgy: 'Our help is in the name of Yahweh, who made heaven and earth' (v. 8). With this, then, we have covered the most important aspects of the religious value of faith in the creation. The creation of *man* is touched upon incidentally in prayer for happiness (Job 10: 8–11), for understanding (Ps 119 (118): 73), or in order to prove God's omniscience (Ps 94 (93): 9, 10), yet the central motives still remain: God's greatness and his power, which make us trust in him. And we hope thus to have said enough about faith in creation in the Old Testament.

The holy scripture of the New Testament

In the books of the New Testament this faith, under the aspects we have described, is not further developed and even hardly expressed in a direct fashion. As long as Jesus and the apostles are speaking before a Jewish audience the doctrine of creation needs just as little emphasis as monotheism. It comes down mainly to the confessing of the Christ as the only Son of God and thus of God himself as the Father, which is in the end expressed by Paul, and at the same time by John, in the relation of them both to the creation itself. It is here worthwhile quoting a

72

passage from Saint Paul in which the ancient faith in creation, together with the new revelation concerning the place of the Son, is expressed, almost in passing, in a discourse on the eating of meat which has been offered to pagan idols. Although heathendom acknowledges many gods and lords, says the apostle, 'yet for us there is one God, the Father, from whom are all things and for whom we exist, and one Lord, Jesus Christ, through whom are all things and through whom we exist' (1 Cor 8:6). This is just about the only text in which the faith in creation by God, the Father, is quite directly expressed, although together with the place of the Son in the creation. The remaining texts in the New Testament books deal directly with this place of the Son. Tradition, in its turn, will also occupy itself with the last point, especially in the struggle against arianism. In an indirect way this conflict also resulted in a more precise formulation of the creation faith as such. For it was in this that the expression 'out of nothing' received more noticeable emphasis, in that the emergence of created reality 'out of nothing' was sharply opposed to the emergence of the Son 'out of the substance of the Father', which may in no sense be called an emergence 'out of nothing'.

Pronouncements of the teaching authority

At this juncture, christian revelation has already long since left the Jewish milieu and with this has come the necessity of explicitly confessing the faith in creation. In fact, the text from Saint Paul which we cited above, already indicates a confrontation with paganism. The latter is opposed to christianity not only in the popular cult of the 'many gods and many lords' (1 Cor 8:5), of which Paul speaks, but also in speculations concerning necessary emanations, two opposed principles, ideas or eons existing beside God. In tracing the church's reaction to this we shall limit ourselves to her official documents. In this case, the first thing we notice is that during the first few centuries the acknowledgement of God as creator begins to slowly find its way into the baptismal symbol of faith, and that as its first article, which receives the well-known form: 'I believe in God, the Father almighty, creator of heaven and earth'. The oldest text of the apostolic symbol, the Latin 'textus Romanus' and the Greek of the 'Psalterium Aethelstani' do not yet contain the addition 'creator of heaven and earth'; but it appears in the 'textus receptus', of which a Latin version is to be found in the so-called 'ordo Romanus' and a Greek one in the writings of Cyril of Jerusalem. This shows that the present-day form of the first article of faith became general in the fourth century.

At the beginning of the next century we find belief in the creation presented for the first time as something to be held *sub anathemate*, by the provincial council of Toledo in 400 (Dz 21). Meanwhile, a more exact formulation of the biblical 'heaven and earth' is added to the various symbols, clearly indicating a campaign against speculations concerning ideas, eons or demiurges which are said to exist independently of God. This is the expression 'of all things, visible and invisible', with which most of us are acquainted from the creed of the ecumenical councils of Nicea and Constantinople (Dz 54 and 86; cf 13 and 19), the Creed of our contemporary mass. In this there lies a rejection of the manichees and priscillians, who maintained an emanation from God of all spiritual reality, a position which was expressly condemned at the provincial council of Braga in 561 (Dz 235). The same council condemns in further detail the dualism of

74

the heretics mentioned, particularly in the following canon: 'If anyone says that the devil was not first a good angel made by God and that his nature was not God's work, but says that he arose out of darkness and has no maker, but is himself the principle and essence of evil, as the manichees and priscillians have said, let him be banned from the community of the church' (Dz 238), and in the canons which condemn the belief that the devil is the creator of bad weather, of the human body in procreation and of all flesh (Dz 238, 241–244).

And with this we have said enough about the more precise formulations of belief in the creation over and against paganism and its infiltrations, in so far as they fall within the Graeco-Roman world and the patristic period. They added nothing essentially new to scripture, but merely formulated certain points more precisely. The same can be said of the doctrinal pronouncements of the church in the centuries following. During this time several points, which up until then had only been expressed on the level of the general and ordinary teaching authority of the church, now become objects of solemn definitions of faith. This occurs first with the condemnation of manichean dualism when it is renewed in the twelfth and thirteenth centuries by the albigensians. Then in 1215 the ecumenical Third Lateran Council expresses belief in the one God in three Persons, who is: 'one unique principle of all things, creator of all things, visible and invisible, the spiritual and the physical, who by his almighty power has from the beginning of time made out of nothing both sorts of creature, the spiritual and the physical, that is, the angelic and the earthly sorts; and finally the human, which is as it were joined together out of spirit and body' (Dz 428). This formulation brought to a close a development in the dogma of the Trinity, which we shall not discuss now. Its intention is clearly to define matter as a creation of the one and only God who also created the spirit, and to confess man, even though he is seen as the *confinium* of the material and spiritual world, as the creature of the same unique God. Little room is left hereby for a dualism between spirit and matter, and there is likewise no place for a principle of evil. The council immediately adds: 'For the devil and the other demons were by their nature created by God as good, but have of themselves become evil. Man, however, has sinned through temptation by the devil' (Dz 428).

The next council to occupy itself with the creation takes place many centuries later. It is the last ecumenical council but one, Vatican I (1869–70). In its consideration of God as creator in the first chapter of its first dogmatic constitution, this council repeats almost the whole of the sentence which we have quoted above from the Lateran Council (Dz 1783). In various canons this belief of the church in creation is more clearly defined over and against materialism and the various forms of pantheism (Dz 1801–5). Of particular importance in this connection is canon 4 (Dz 1804), which contrasts creation to an emanation from God, or an evolution or self-manifestation by which the divine being becomes everything, or self-determination by which undetermined reality becomes world. Nor is it less important that in this council the teaching authority speaks for the first time, and with insistence, of the motive and the freedom of God's act of creation. In fact, the sentence which the Vatican Council borrows from the Lateran is completed in various ways. The Council of the Lateran said that God created 'by his almighty power', that of the Vatican says 'by his goodness and his almighty power' (Dz 1783). This is clarified by the words which immediately follow: 'not in order to increase his happiness, nor in order to acquire his perfection, but to show these by the good that he imparts to his creatures' (Dz 1783). It is stated further on that God creates by virtue of a decision that is free in the highest possible way, 'liberrimo consilio' (Dz 1783). These two points are summed up together with the fact of creation itself in the following canon: 'If anyone does not confess that the world and all that it contains, spiritual and material, has in its whole substance been brought forth out of nothing by God—or says that God did not create with a will that is free from all necessity, but as necessarily as he loves himself;—or denies that the world has been created to the glory of God;—let him be anathema' (Dz 1805). Thus on the one side goodness, on the other freedom. In addition, for God goodness itself is ultimately not something by which he is compelled. This is pointed out in the encyclical *Humani generis*, when it brands as error or at least in danger of error the proposition that 'the creation of the world is necessary, because it results out of the necessary generosity of the divine love' (n. 25).

This brings us to the end of our presentation of the sources. We ended our treatment of the Old Testament with an indication of the religious value of the doctrine of creation, and to this we shall now add a few further thoughts. In itself, creation inspired the Old Testament writers to the praising of God's majesty. We find this once more in the Vatican definition that the world was created to the glory of God. In the Old Testament, however, the strongest emphasis is on the connection between creation and covenant: our God, Yahweh, is the creator; our help is in the name of Yahweh, who made heaven and earth. It is in following the path set by special-isation of the development of dogma that the church now speaks mostly about creation as such. But in doing this she nevertheless still uses ideas which were first of all revealed to us in connection with the covenant and the redemption, namely freedom and love. Not only are God's covenant with Israel and his calling Abraham free, but also his calling man and world out of nothing. But above all these are deeds of goodness, of love. God's glory does not consist in his seeking applause, but in his 'showing his perfection by the good·that he imparts to his creatures'. In its turn, belief in the creation has already become 'belief in the love God has for us' (1 Jn 4: 16). This invites us to consider further the relations between creation and covenant, which is what we shall do in our next chapter. First, however, we shall in the following section explain the actual idea of creation in more detail.

2 A more detailed consideration of creation

In the preceding section we let the whole range of sources speak directly. In doing this we not only repeatedly heard the acknowledgement that God is the creator of heaven and earth, but also already penetrated to its meaning. We shall try in this section to define more precisely and explain more systematically that meaning, that content. We do not intend to repeat ourselves, for there still remain various questions which do not find an answer in the sources, but which are nevertheless within the limits we have set ourselves in the discussion of this first article of faith (for we shall deal later with the one concerning the relation of the creation to Christ). Even in replying to these questions, however, we hope to continue thinking on the lines of what we have drawn from scripture and tradition, so as not to build a merely logical speculation but to remain within the religious context which we have sketched.

78

Three points will be dealt with in this way. First we shall attempt to give a more detailed description of God's creation itself. Subsequently we shall compare God's creative activity with other deeds of his which may be said to concern the world but not to belong to his covenant activity. These are the maintenance and government of his creation. Finally, we shall define the relation of all these divine activities to those of creatures themselves, so as to see how they do not limit each other exclusively, nor even mutually.

God's creative activity

Creation is an act of God by which 'heaven and earth, all things visible and invisible', or 'the world', i.e., all finite reality, all that exists apart from God, receives its existence. When this act of God is described in more detail, then for our natural reason and for God's own word of revelation alike there is only one way open, that which proceeds from the activities by which something arises, in some way gets existence, here on earth. These activities are of many sorts. Usually, they are only described in a general way, and a few general characteristics of earthly activity are pointed out in order to see, by means of the way of negation, how exalted God's creative act is above them. This is undoubtedly a correct method, for in the end everything comes down to the fundamental difference between all earthly activity and God's creation. However, we shall associate ourselves more with the doctrine of creation already seen in scripture and tradition if we first make an effort to list the various types of earthly activity and then briefly compare them with God's act of creation. By doing so we shall probably also obtain a more concrete idea of the immeasurable difference between the activities of this earth and those of God.

79

It has perhaps been noticed that we are talking about *earthly* activities, not human ones. The reason being that even in the events, activities or influences that occur below man one can find a starting-point for comparison with God's creative deed. This is done by saying, for example, that all that exists in this world has God as the source from which it flows forth. Such modes of speech are to be found among christian philosophers, theologians and mystics, and are even not uncommon there. Yet we must be fully aware that they are foreign to scripture; that, on the contrary, the biblical doctrine of creation expresses itself most precisely in the image of an activity that differs radically from them, namely that of the spoken command of a person, and also that ecclesiastical usage is not favourable towards terms such as 'flowing forth' (*emanatio*) and that it conceives of expressions like 'out of nothing' and 'out of God' as contraries. We hope to return presently to this point in more detail; for the moment suffice it to say that if we are going to speak of God as source, this manner of representation must be clearly understood.

Let us now turn to the *human* activities through which something arises. The first sort we meet is work, by which something is fabricated. An image of this usually appears to most of us when we look more closely at the notion of God's 'making the world', and the bible also calls up such a picture each time it brings 'God's hands' into his creation in one way or another. The difference between human work and divine creation is most clearly brought out in the fact that the former always fabricates its product 'out of something else', while God creates 'out of nothing'. Human work only brings something forth in a new state, and precisely for this reason it does not create, but only changes. It causes qualitative or even substantial changes, and for our outward perception only quantitative alterations. This in spite of all the nobility of human work, is its poverty as compared to God's creation.

Human work can be achieved in two basic ways. Firstly by instruments, which may, as machines, have a certain independence. The bible will be found rarely to use this technical activity as an image of God's creative deed; the only comparison one can mention in this connection is that of the potter, and even this is not elaborated upon in an analysis of the technical side of the activity. If we were to do this, however, then the expression 'out of nothing' could be completed by adding 'with nothing'. God creates without materials and also without instruments. At another, higher level, human work is achieved when its result is made the expression of the human spirit, especially when this occurs in an artistic way. One could find a comparison of God's creation with artistic production in Psalm 19 (18), in which created reality 'tells', 'proclaims' and 'speaks'. Such artistic production is designated in English and in many other languages by the same word that is used for God's activity: 'creation'. It is also the human activity whose product is strikingly new with respect to material or instrument; precisely in being the expression of the spirit it has something of a 'creation out of nothing'. And yet here true talent or genius expresses itself partly in the skill with which the 'creator' adapts himself to the requirements of material and instruments. And above all, even the idea which is expressed is first 'received', 'conceived', while of God it is truly said: 'Who has been the Lord's counsellor?'

By referring to human activities we have entered the world of the person as such, the world of inter-personal relations. Here one person can create situations of striking originality for another—here again the word 'creation') even though they are firmly established in a juridical order. Perhaps the reason for this is that for 'create' Latin uses a verb which signifies raising to an office, namely 'creare', and Greek the verb 'to found' (a city, etc.), *ktizein*. However this may be, even the bible itself, in Genesis 1 and Psalm 33 (32), chooses an interpersonal activity as starting-point, that of calling, commanding, the speaking of words. It is obvious that here all corporeity must be eliminated, and therefore the making of air vibrations by movement of the vocal chords, making sound; although in fact the sacred author shows little concern about this. It was essentially a matter of indicating that God enters upon his creative act freely and in sovereign manner, as the personal living God, as Lord. Here we may once again note the contrast with images such as source or foundation. In the first place, however, it must be noticed that in this personal activity of God not only are material and instrument, idea and counsellor missing, but there is also no partner in the dialogue, no person called upon. God does not call a being, he calls into being, he calls out of nothing.

We have now reviewed a whole series of earthly points of comparison with God's creative activity. One might stop at this point, but yet another human activity demands our attention, namely reproduction, or rather, the procreation of a new human being. Ideally considered, this act, with the whole of its context, is the summit of physical achievement and of interpersonal communion at the same time, but pre-eminently it gives existence to a person. That is why we must also consider this human activity as comparable to the divine act of creation. When one finds the mother of the Macchabees talking about her maternal task of bearing, feeding and educating her son, and subsequently about God's creation out of nothing (2 Macch 7:27ff.), one may perhaps think one has found a scriptural comparison of this sort. The more natural interpretation, however, is that she is recalling the memory of her motherhood only or mainly in order to secure her son's obedience, as appears from her opening words: 'My son, have pity on me' (ibid.). At all events, nowhere else in the bible is God's creation compared with human propagation, and such a comparison is certainly alien to tradition as expressed in its official documents. In the bible this probably finds its explanation in the fact that Israel's image of God, in contrast to that of the pagans, is completely asexual. A god who generates the world would immediately suggest the idea of a goddess together with him and of beings in the world which have the nature of children of the gods, and both of these notions are at variance with the monotheism of revelation. Thus we may take generation as comparable to God's creative activity, but must once more purify the idea radically—while other points of comparison are much closer at hand. Moreover, there appears to be another reason why this comparison is not useful here and which explains why it has been shunned by tradition. For human procreation was used for comparison in the revelation of a much greater mystery than creation, that of the holy Trinity. And so we shall limit ourselves here to the conclusion that God's creation also surpasses human generation, in that it requires no collaboration and implies nothing in the nature of a fragmentation of God's being.

And so we would restrict ourselves to the other earthly activities, in particular the human, which may serve as terms of comparison with the creation. Surveying them all together, we may say, in scholastic terms, that those activities or influences which are a form of or show a connection with material causality are used less by revelation (if they are used at all) and are less suited, and therefore, conversely, require a much greater correction than all that refers to an efficient causality. Thus we may add that among the forms of efficient causality it is above all personal activity, and in particular that of spoken command, that deserves preference in the drawing of such comparison.

Now let us compare earthly activities in general with God's creation so that we may describe the latter more accurately by seeing the difference between the two. It is noticeable that man, when he brings something forth, is always surrounded by persons and things which are also concerned in his activity. God, however, stands alone, and this provides us with a first definition of the idea of creation: the bringing forth of something by God alone. Since 1948 the new Dutch catechism has taken this definition as its starting-point. While formerly God's title of 'creator of heaven and earth' was explained by saying that God 'brought forth everything out of nothing' (old catechism, q. 37), the new catechism states that he is called the creator because he made everything by his almighty will alone. This is completely in keeping with Genesis 1 and Psalm 33 (32), as will be seen from what we said above about these texts. It may be noted, moreover, that this seems a good definition, because it expresses God's creation and nothing more. For our human fabrication never takes place solely through our spiritual-physical substance, let alone through our will. On the other hand, God's gift of grace to his creature not only proceeds from God, but presupposes the creature as the receiving party; and the Father's bringing forth of the Son and Spirit is not a case of 'making'. So in the activity of creation God is the only maker, and

84

not through a body that is essentially part of a co-operating world around us, but through his act of will. Here we must therefore clarify the idea of 'making' by adding 'by his will alone', which the bible did by using the symbol of God's word of command.

This continues to be of importance when we wish to use the idea of 'cause'. We have acquired this notion from the workings of the world, and in fact primarily from material processes. Thus here also all dependence on other beings must be denied and only the pure activity preserved. If we wish to apply this idea to God, then it may correctly be said that he is the cause of all things, the first cause, the cause of all causes outside himself, and that only in him is there causality which is free from the characteristic of being itself caused, the characteristic of all causality among creatures. Nevertheless, it can be readily understood that people sometimes refuse to use the idea of 'cause' in referring to God. Here the concept is being restricted to this world and its level of reality, whereas God's activity is at least personal. Thus it is already clear that the idea of cause must be thoroughly cleansed, and this is even more necessary when God is referred to as 'source', 'foundation' or something similar. We have already pointed out that the biblical symbol stands right at the other end of the scale of earthly causalities, that of personal intention. And for this reason the Creator can also—and to this degree—be known from his creation as the 'personal God', as the encyclical *Humani generis* asserts.

Moreover, even when in this connection one wishes to take man's personal will as starting-point, the idea must be purged of any aspect of determination, external or internal. This is clear from the words we quoted in the preceding section from

Vatican 1 and *Humani generis*: 'liberrimo consilio', 'with a will that is free from all necessity', and therefore not 'as necessarily as He loves himself', nor 'out of the necessary generosity of the divine love'. Here one can see a difference from the procession of the Son and the Holy Spirit out of the Father, in which necessity and freedom coincide in the most sublime way and which may thus be said to occur 'as necessarily as God loves himself' and 'out of the necessary generosity of the divine love'. The intention of these pronouncements, however, was not to show the difference between the creation of the world and the bringing forth of the divine persons, but to reject a mistaken doctrine concerning creation itself. In doing this Vatican 1 had the semi-christianised idealism of Günther in mind.

In the canon preceding this condemnation of a necessary creation, the council had condemned even stronger assertions of such a creation; namely, that which denies the distinction between creator and creature in a pantheistic way (Dz 1804) and the teaching 'that finite reality, both corporeal and spiritual, or at least the spiritual, flowed forth (*emanasse*) from the divine substance'. This further condemnation of pantheistic emanation is also of importance here. Although the phrase 'emanation from God' has certainly appeared more than once in traditional christian usage, the idea nevertheless needs once more to be thoroughly cleansed, not only of all material causality with respect to God, but also of all determination. In the interests of clarity, therefore, it is better to avoid using the term. And this is even true of the preposition 'from'. The fact that God alone gives existence may in itself be expressed by saying that all things are 'from God', and indeed St Paul sometimes speaks in this way (1 Cor 8:6; Rm 11:36). But in ecclesiastical usage since the struggle against arianism 'out of nothing' has been the accepted expression for the origin of creation, whilst the Son proceeds 'from the substance of the Father', and when one uses this term for the world there is again a danger that one will be denying the real creation. With this we hope to have said enough concerning the definition of God's creation as the making of all things 'by his almighty will alone'.

The negation that was indicated above by the word 'alone' is more strongly emphasised in a second definition, which we have already given and which can be put briefly as: *creating is making out of nothing*. This already implies, in connection with our previous definition, an explanation: 'nothing' is not presented here as a positive starting-point, a preceding stage of events or of matter; it is rather the negation of all this. Thus 'out of nothing' means 'not out of something', because only from God (in so far as there can be talk of anything coming 'from' God). Following what we said earlier, the 'out of nothing' can be completed by saying: out of, with the aid of, and by means of nothing, and at the same time: with and through no one apart from God. Likewise we may add: calling, bringing forth out of nothing. In this way the terms of these two conceptual definitions are seen to be already clear from what has previously been said.

However, there is another way in which they may be illuminated, namely by asking whether or not they are in a certain sense applicable to earthly, in particular human making, thereby more accurately defining the sense in which they are used with regard to God. In fact we ourselves do make things out of nothing. For what has been made did not exist previously, otherwise nothing would have arisen through our making. Thus in comparison with the entire result of our fabrication there was previously nothing, nothing of precisely that which we made. But there was no absence of material, and this is precisely the nothing out of which God creates. Scholasticism expresses this by saying that we make something only 'ex nihilo sui', God, in contrast, creates it 'ex nihilo sui et subiecti'.

The meaning of this may be made clear in either of two ways: by proceeding from the poverty or from the richness inherent in our productive activity. Emphasising the poverty, we may say that all our making is only the changing of something else, as we asserted above when we took work and craftsmanship as starting-points in our consideration of God's creation. God, however, does not change something in order to create; the whole world, with all the changes which are contained within it, arose in its entirety without change through God's creation.

When we now refer to the richness of our production, as we did in the case of expressive production or artistic 'creation', as it is called, we must point out the astonishing difference between the result and that which precedes it, in one word, the newness of that result. The fact that our productions are not 'ex nihilo subiecti' reduces our making to a changing, but this changing nevertheless brings about something that is 'ex nihilo sui', and therefore new. And the result is all the more new in the measure that the spirit expresses itself more strongly and personally therein: think, for instance, of technical and artistic products. Now with God, the result of his creation has a complete and all-comprehending newness; in so far as it arises through him, the world is 'brand-new', it has not taken over or continued anything old. It might be said that the latter term has no sense here, since we only recognise the new by comparison with the old, and apart from God and creation there

88

is no point of reference to be used in making a judgement about the world. To us, however, it seems better to speak of the quite unique sense which the term 'newness' takes on in creation, as also do 'beginning' and 'origin'. All these terms point to the creature's orientation towards God and nothing apart from him, and therefore refer to creation metaphorically rather than literally. And yet we need such terminology in order to reveal the completely unique character of creation as fully as possible and in order that when we perceive newness in the world, we shall be referred by it to creation. Finally, one might say that the statement 'creation is utterly and completely new' just as much refers to God by way of an absence of 'other things' as the statement 'creation is out of nothing'. And so this completely unique newness provides us with a last attempt at re-expressing the 'ex nihilo' in more detail.

So far we have discussed two definitions of creation which express the wholly unique nature of God's activity in ways which are essentially negative: 'by God's will alone' and 'out of nothing'. There is, however, a third definition of the concept, one which sees creation primarily in the creature itself, and thereby sounds more positive. It follows from each of the preceding definitions. When we make something, not alone, but with others, by means of other things and certainly out of something else, we do not hold responsibility for the whole reality of the product, we have not brought it forth in all the aspects of its reality. When, on the contrary, God makes something 'by his almighty will alone' and 'out of nothing', then he makes it in the whole of its reality. Thus creation may now also be defined as: *the making of something in the whole of its reality.*

Here it may first be emphasised that the whole

reality of the creature, no single element or aspect excepted, is the result of the creative activity of God. This we may also express by talking of its reality as such, its being, not as this or that, but simply its being as being. And so our third definition of creation is also provided by the scholastic formula: the making of a being as being. Those who are at all familiar with scholastic terminology will remember that the object of rational knowledge is referred to in the same words: being as being. We might now join these two definitions by saying that God's creation is always an address to reason, reason as such, and thus it has a verbal character as described in Psalm 19 (18)—and that, conversely, rational knowledge is always an acknowledgement of the creature as creature and thus of the creator in his creature.

But let us return to the actual activity of creation. The reality which results from it can be seen not only in all its content and comprehensiveness, but subsequently also in its depth, its foundation, its substance. For if the whole reality of a created thing is from the creator, this means that the thing comes from him not only according to certain aspects or modes of being, but as it exists in itself. This is why the classical expression of our third definition of creation reads: the making of something according to the whole of its substance. The First Vatican Council takes over this definition, together with that of 'making out of nothing' when it says in one of its canons: 'If anyone does not confess that the world and all that it contains, spiritual and material, has in its whole substance been brought forth out of nothing by God . . . let him be anathema.' This third definition is also—when once more 'make' is used in contrast to the bringing forth of the Son by the Father—an authentic definition of creation. For we ourselves can make something not only accord-

90

ing to one of its accidental modalities, but according to its substance—yet never according to the whole of its substance, seeing that in doing so we require other substances as our material starting-point. Furthermore, the produced substance is new and different with respect to the producer. This becomes especially clear in the bringing forth of a new living being, which is new and different with respect to the parent beings. But this is realised in the highest way in the generation of man, who as a person is so radically new and different that precisely in this spiritual, personal nature he escapes the productive act of his parents. But man is a creature of God even in so far as he is a spiritual person, in fact it is precisely as a person that he is most the creature of God. In man God is most fully the creator of the whole substance and of the particular substance of the person, in an act which surpasses all human making, even human generation. God is the creator of all things according to the whole of their substance and of all human beings according to the whole of their personality. His creation is a making and calling out of nothing of that which in the first place is unmakeable as far as we are concerned and can only be called by us when it already exists, and herein lies the summit of creation. God's final achievement on the sixth day not only constitutes the crown above all his other creatures, it is also the most sublime deed of his creation. We might therefore extend our third and last definition thus: creating is making the world according to the whole substance of all it contains, as far as and including man, for whom it exists and in whom it finds its coherence.

Our consideration of the act of creation starting from several points of comparison in this world and from a few definitions has now been carried sufficiently far for the moment. In concluding the first point in this section we should like for a little while to give our attention to the result of the activity of creation, i.e., to 'creation' in the passive sense: created reality; this we shall consider precisely in so far as it is created. Let us begin by establishing that this nature of being created is connected with the whole existence, the whole reality of the creature, which it permeates completely and utterly. By saying this we are only repeating in a different manner the last definition we developed above: creating is making something in the whole of its reality, the whole of its substance. This is briefly put, but it cannot be stressed enough. 'The creature, in all that it is, is of God,' says St Thomas in his concise way. Not a single element or moment of it exists without dependence on the creator; and no single aspect of it can be thought of in a concrete manner if it is not thought of as created, including even its peculiarity, its substance, and its freedom. Presently we shall see the consequences of this.

First, it is also necessary to consider created reality from the opposite view in order to develop this point. We say—and we must likewise say this on account of our faith in the creation—that this being, which in the whole of its reality is dependent and created, nevertheless also has its own individuality, its independence, its personality, its freedom. Indeed, we believe that it is even possible to say that the creature has all this not in spite of the fact that it is a creature, but precisely because of its complete dependence on the creator and by virtue of his creative deed. Belief in the creation teaches us to assent to the reality of God and to that of the world with equal firmness. For our natural thought tends towards the dilemma: God or the world, whether in consideration of all being or with regard to certain domains thereof. This dilemma, however, always proceeds from one of the two causes which we cited from the encyclical *Humani generis* at the beginning of this chapter: an exclusive attachment to sensory categories in our thought and the latter's warping by the sinful will. Now faith in the creation saves our natural metaphysic from this dilemma. As is understandable, this faith in scripture and tradition is most directly expressed when the reality of the creature is overemphasised at the cost of the creator, as occurs in all sorts of forms of pantheism and pan-entheism. For the forms of pantheism which were condemned by the First Vatican Council and according to which reality emanates from God's substance, or God's essence becomes everything in a self-manifestation and self-development, or God determines himself from undetermined to all things (Dz 1804), devalue the reality of this world just as much as more 'religious' forms of acosmism do. Because in both God is the 'real thing', the 'universal', and the creature merely a particularisation, an appearance, yes, even an illusion (*maya*). When a christian takes issue against this, in the background there stands his faith in the reality of the flesh of God's Son, but at the same time he is thereby expressing all that we have read in Genesis 1 about the creative power of God's word of command and the concise statements of Psalm 33 (32): 9, 'For he spoke, and it came to be; he commanded, and it stood forth'.

God's creation and his other activities

The creature is, in the whole of its reality, of God and nothing is withheld from dependence upon him. And on the other hand: God wills, he creates, he realises the whole creature, he causes it to become fully itself. These two truths will form the starting-points of the two themes which await discussion in this section: the relation of the creation to the other activities of God, such as the maintenance and government of the world, and the relation of the creation, together with these other activities, to the individuality of the creature's own activity. The first of these points is a development of the truth that the creature is in the whole of its reality something of God. In this light a unity may be indicated between the creation, maintenance and government which we so spontaneously distinguished, a unity, however, which cannot injure all the richness of nuance within this distinction.

At first sight the distinction is a distinction in time. The Dutch catechism expresses this by saying: 'After the creation God maintains and governs the world' (q. 26). This is in keeping with the order in the book of Genesis, of which the creation story constitutes the beginning, and with the whole usage of scripture and tradition, according to which: *in the beginning* God *created* the world. Let us start by noting that this mode of representation is certainly objective, in so far as the order of events cannot be reversed. For the creation must be presupposed because it relates to the existence, the substance of the world itself; whilst maintenance and government relate to its duration and activity. Because 'God maintains the world means: through his almighty power God causes it to continue' (ibid., q. 27), and 'God governs the world means: God leads everything to the end for which He has created the world' (ibid., q. 28).

Nevertheless, could not the priority of creation also be conceived of otherwise, and probably more deeply than as a temporal precedence? When from describing maintenance and government we return to creation, how can we differentiate this from those other activities? One may say in this case: by creation God gives the *first* being, the *beginning*, he

94

makes the creature; as theologians sometimes say, 'with a certain newness of being: *cum quadam novitate essendi*'. We have already pointed out that this beginning and this newness are of a completely unique nature, since an actual point of comparison would have to be situated in a temporal reality outside creation, and this is something that precisely does not exist. Thus we might perhaps also say that the world is something that not only is created, but also becomes created, a beginning out of God's omnipotence, a newness out of his originality. It may perhaps be objected that only the first existence, the beginning of the world was 'out of nothing' in the usual sense of that expression. Yet even this does not seem to us a convincing argument for placing creation and maintenance before and after each other. For creation as a whole is at every instant of its occurrence out of nothing and under this aspect the beginning of its existence is in no way privileged, because 'nothing' did not precede creation. It therefore seems that neither terms such as 'beginning' and 'newness' nor creation 'out of nothing' give us a criterion for distinguishing the creation of the world from its maintenance and government.

When we now finally turn to the third definition of creation which we set up, we find that this pleads most of all for the identification of all these activities of God concerning the world. For creation, we said, is the making of something in the whole of its reality. If God creates, then he makes everything continually, he makes everything just as much in its continuation as in its origin. Indeed, this is even a characteristic which distinguishes God's creation from our making just as much as the 'out of nothing' aspect does. It is precisely because nothing outside God is answerable for creation that its dependence upon him is total under all aspects, including its duration. Our artefacts continue without our aid, and even children grow independently of their parents, physically and spiritually. As regards God, however, with each further step in self-development the creature at the same time becomes more dependent, more 'brought forth' (and at the same time more itself). And thus in this way also, creation, maintenance and government seem to coincide. If any distinction may still be drawn, it lies not in a succession but in the fact that creation is the all-comprehending activity, which contains maintenance and government of the world within it as aspects of itself. Maintenance is creation in so far as it concerns the duration of the creature, government the same in so far as it concerns its activity. But both *are* creation.

Here is our unity. But we have also already said that the richness of nuance in our distinction must not be lost. If the distinction according to temporal succession may be reduced to a representation and thereby an expression of the unity of God's activity 'up until now' (Jn 5: 17)—an expression which is both beautiful and necessary for us—there is nevertheless another dimension in which the creation can be delimited from God's other works and in which this is in fact done in the pronouncements of the church. Within the world itself we see everything changing and developing itself. This means that there is a continuous movement, but also the discontinuity of the jump. What arises can be explained in terms of what already existed, of what is old; but never completely, and in this measure it is new.

Newness, spring, youth are just as much the content of our observation and experience as presevation and stability. When one enters the domain of scientific statement, however, especially when it is given quantitative expression, one tends to leave that which is new out of one's considerations as much as possible because newness as such is not eligible for explanation within creation itself. But this does not change the fact that our experience of newness is as objective as that of stability. Even when quantitatively the new may be reduced to the old, as in the case of the law of the conservation of energy, the change in the form of this energy still brings forth something new qualitatively—and in fact even quantitatively. In the sphere of life every individual has his own exclusive plan of development. Above this, the person has the newness of being able, in a free decision which is always made completely in his or her own way, to indicate, accept or also to reject his or her own lot and all that is 'pre-established'. Thus as one climbs the scale of creation there is an ever greater newness. It does not consist of 'new pieces' which are added from without, but lies embedded in the development of the old itself. In every development, fulfilment, or completion there always lies a surprise. It is already present in the circular process of nature; how much more in history, which we contrasted with the course of nature in our preceding chapter precisely because of this 'more'.

Now it is precisely this newness that we can ascribe each time to God's creation. Newness thus always goes together with the maintenance, moving and leading of existing creatures in their self-development. It is no more purely added on to God's other activities than totally foreign elements appear within this world. On the contrary, the new creation is connected with maintenance, etc., indeed, it is even rooted therein, because the new really comes forth out of the old, the higher evolves out of the lower and the child is brought forth by its parents. But on the other hand this new creation is also distinct from maintenance and movement, precisely because from out of the old there comes something new, something higher, a new living being, a new person. The new creation does not exist as something different standing apart from this maintenance, but is an opposing moment in it, just as newness is not something apart from the possibility of explanation in terms of the old, but an opposed moment in the being that arises out of the old.

In this sentence we hope to have basically purified the idea of 'new creation' from the quantitative 'creating something thereby'. It may be applied thus in the sphere of life, certainly with respect to the arising of new species and, in fact, to each individual. The latter is certainly the case on the human level, where the individual is a person. Thus man is created in his personal nature as such, which is what the church teaches under the doctrine of the infusion or immediate creation of the soul. We do not intend to treat this point in detail here. However, this truth may be remembered as the conclusion of our comparison between the creation and the other divine activities mentioned. Human parents are father and mother of the whole of their child—not only of his body—yet in that child the spiritual soul is independent of them in a direct way. So also God works through maintenance and movement in the whole of their generating activity and at the same time the spiritual soul, and thereby the person, is created new and immediately therein. This origin of the human person gives the highest and clearest example of the way in which God's creation is always distinguished from yet unified with his maintenance and government of the world.

God's activity and ours

In a third and final point we have now to discuss the relation between all these activities of the creator on the one hand and the creature's own activities on the other. Here an important place will be taken by the reflection which we developed at the end of our second point. This was: by his creation God gives the creature reality and individuality, independence and personality. What we said earlier in terms of being can now be repeated in terms of activity. This activity comes utterly and completely from God, as does the whole of the creature's being. It is completely dependent on and brought about by God's all-comprehending causation. But it nevertheless holds true that through this total causation God makes the creature act completely as itself, according to its own nature and norm, so that the result is truly brought forth by that very activity. Here again belief in creation solves the dilemma: God or the world. Just as it is opposed to acosmism, in complete or weakened form, so it is here to all forms of occasionalism. For the christian, the world is no more a mere occasion for what is 'actually' and exclusively the activity of God, than it is an illusion.

In saying this it must none the less be remembered that in the domain of activity the dilemma 'God or world' thrusts itself upon us with more force than in the domain of being as such. For our wanting to set ourselves up in our activity as autonomous with respect to God is precisely characteristic of our sinfulness. The first reaction to this—though not the deepest, nor the most fully converted—is to underestimate the value of human activity before God. And more than anything else: because all our thought has its roots in the sensible world, in thinking about the activity of God and creature we must continually wrestle free from representations such as two horses drawing one cart, and the like. For in the field of physical action it holds true that what one does another need not do, and vice versa. In the relation between God and creature, however, God does not act at the cost of the activity of the creature, the creature at the cost of God's activity. To tell the truth, in fact, what we said about physical action no longer holds completely true as soon as one introduces the mind, the spirit. For if with his mind man is to let his physical activity complete or replace nature, a technical invention is needed which, as far as one human mind on its own is concerned, demands a much greater achievement than in a situation in which he works without technical help. A similarly great achievement is demanded in a more constant way when one human being leads the work of others.

All this, however, is but a weak shadow of the relation of God's activity to that of his creatures. Here he is the one who does everything, by giving creatures all their activity, by making it real, by allowing creatures, or better, by causing them, to act in everything. But God also makes the creature itself act, he realises the creature itself as acting under its own power and according to its own laws and as itself causing the result, its activity. Although for the relation between the actions of two creatures, at least in so far as they are physical, it may be true that what the one does the other need not do, and thus also that what one does more the other needs to do less, when it comes to the relation between God and creature there can be no such talk. On the contrary, there it is the case that what God does, the creature also does; what God does not do, neither does the creature; that which God does more, the creature also does more; that which God does less, the creature also does less.

It is worth going a little more closely into the realisation of this general principle in the various spheres and forms of created activity. In the first part of this section we have already discussed how in the making or bringing forth of something, the product always manifests a newness which comes from God's creation, as opposed to his maintenance and government. On the other hand, however, the new thing comes forth out of the old; even the human person is the child of his parent. This last aspect now needs to be emphasised. Divine activity, even in its creative moment, in no way eliminates production by the creature. This holds true of individuals in that parenthood is always a reality, even among human beings. And in so far as science establishes transition between the species of living beings, evolution, it also holds there. An evolution which is accepted as final principle of explanation is obviously at variance with belief in creation, but an evolution within a created world is not. On one condition, however: that here also creation of that which is new must be accepted, which in concrete terms means that man in his personal nature, in other words, the spiritual soul of man, is not explained in terms of the lower species. With this enough has been said about the making and bringing forth of a new being. Let us now say something particularly about created activity, in so far as it is physical and in so far as it is spiritual, all the time in relation to God's all-inclusive causation.

Inasmuch as it is physical or bound up with the physical, activity within this world is characterised by regularity. We say 'inasmuch as it is physical or bound up with the physical' because there are not only physical, chemical and biological, but also economic and psychological laws. A law formulates a particular constant in an activity. It is of importance to notice, however, how precisely it formulates this constant. In our opinion too little content is ascribed to laws when they are seen exclusively as statistical statements of the chances of the occurrence of certain phenomena. Undoubtedly, for every law one can give the percentage of times that it holds and that of its exceptions, even though the latter may be as small a fraction as 1 per cent. In itself, however, the law states something truly general, although not the complete generality of a certain phenomenon, since then the percentage of exceptions would be zero. One may, we believe, synthesise these two aspects by saying that a law provides us with an objectively justified expectation of a certain phenomenon, because it refers in a completely general way to a force, a cause which of itself brings forth this phenomenon. The phenomenon will thus also appear thereby—except when other forces neutralise the force in question and so prevent its action. It is therefore better to formulate a law by saying: this tends to bring about a certain phenomenon, than by saying: this brings about that phenomenon.

This discussion of the nature of a law serves to make more clear to us that God's activity in the world also continues to bring its laws to full expression. Here there remains the distinction between the creation and the remaining works of God which we drew in the previous reflection. This says that a law is never the complete explanation of a fact, that there is always an aspect of newness bound up with it which cannot be subsumed under the law, however accurately one may define it. But on the other hand the law holds, because this creation of the new is wholly part of a regularity. An example of this is that even the creation of the spiritual soul of man is quite harmoniously bound up with the laws of human generation and does not interrupt their realisation. God's freedom in creating and maintaining is in the first place the freedom with which he chose this world and remains faithful to his own choice in its laws. This is also true of their exceptions, in which the force or cause to which the law refers is in no way absent, only prevented or hindered in its action by other factors. It even holds for the miracle. We mention this separately here, because the essence of the miracle does not consist exclusively in its exceptional character, but also, and primarily, in its value as a sign. We shall discuss this later, however. Suffice it to say here that in miracles the law plays its part in the same way as in natural exceptions. For it is integrated not simply in a different, but in an even higher set of activities. Some miracles manifest the laws of nature in a new way; for example, miracles of healing do not commonly surpass the possibilities of natural cure, but accelerate and force the process in a way not achievable with ordinary forces. That is to say there enter into the situation forces from God. But even these in their turn do not need to be thought of as added to existing creation in a purely extrinsic manner, for even here hidden forces or as yet unrealised combinations can be used, and it even seems to us that this is usually the case. We would once more draw attention to the fact that here the most characteristic quality of the miracle has not been mentioned; that lies in its being a sign and a message. But we have discussed it only in order to show that God's activity in the world respects its laws, or rather, realises the world according to its laws.

But now a word about the higher world of the spirit. In so far as it is spiritual, activity is characterised by freedom. We say 'in so far as it is spiritual' because in our human activity the bond with corporeality will also bring regularity with it once more, which is why we referred above to economic and psychological laws. By this we are already suggesting that freedom is opposed to regularity, to uniformity. This is in the first instance realised in the fact that man is not forced into a particular act by certain circumstances, that in the same circumstances he can always realise various possibilities (and leave others unrealised), that he can *choose*. This capacity to choose remains with freedom throughout our earthly life, for even in the limit-cases where only one possible act remains open to a man—at least as far as the observation of others is concerned—he still continues to stand before the choice of whether to inwardly accept or reject this situation of necessity, or rather, whether to inwardly affirm or deny his relation to God and his fellow men. In this capacity to choose, however, is seen the most basic revelation of self-determination, activity from within, the spontaneity of the person with regard to all it recognises within itself as sense and task.

Now all this is completely and utterly under the influence of God's universal maintaining and governing causation, whilst it nevertheless remains what it is, freedom. God's causation does not make man less free, but from within makes him freely choose and decide. It is above all in this domain that our theology needs to protect itself from the dilemma, God or creature, and continue to affirm: God and creature. This has been especially urgent since the reformation, not only in external disputes but also within the catholic camp itself in those disputes which we touched upon when we spoke, in our first chapter, of God's eternity. We can once more say, with more reason now than then, that the very existence of a problem must here be denied. With Calvin and Bañez we must postulate that God does everything, but at the same time maintain with Molina that man decides wholly and of himself, for evil as well as for good. Here we are touching upon an insight that will be recognised as fundamental in the doctrine on co-operation with grace and on sin and conversion. We shall therefore not discuss it fully, but merely touch upon the relation between God and sin.

Even below the world of the person, disharmony, failure and decay, pain and death are seen, but all of this may hardly be termed evil in so far as in man it is bound up with his sinful state, for sin is the most intense form of evil. Yet, like a shadow, this 'physical evil' shows how with all the activity on God's part, that of the creature is still proper to it in the measure that it may fail. This only becomes fully clear in the world of the person. There, just as in order to explain the origin of the soul a creation by God must be distinguished from his general continuing causation, so from this in its turn there must be distinguished his *permission* in order to explain the existence of evil. On the other hand, however, the creation of the soul is completely taken up as a moment in the other activity of God and such is also the case with the permitting of evil.

We believe that the scriptural manner of expression concerning this question may be synthesised according to the above consideration. In the Old Testament God's working and leading come strongly to the forefront, whilst created causes often go unmentioned; which is why sin is sometimes presented as purely and simply willed and brought about by God. Typical of this is the story of the plagues of Egypt, in which it is mentioned several times that Pharaoh remained obstinate, but also at least eight times that Yahweh hardened Pharaoh's heart (Ex 4:21; 7:3; 9:12; 10:1, 20, 27; 11:10; 14:8). Even the New Testament recalls this by saying 'he hardens the heart of whomever he wills' (Rm 9: 18). Although a little further on we read that this is an 'endurance' on the part of God, even if it is because 'he desires to show his wrath and to make known his power' (Rm 9: 22). The positive willing of sin, however, has above all God's mercy as its end, as the apostle finally says in that incomparable sentence: 'For God has consigned all men to disobedience, that he may have mercy upon all' (Rm 11: 32). He can immediately and with reason add: 'O the depth of the riches and wisdom and knowledge of God! How unsearchable are his judgements and how inscrutable his ways!' (Rm 11: 33). For here we stand confounded by the mystery of God and creature, which in sin reveals its most profound obscurity.

This much is clear, however: God's desiring evil is not directed towards the evil itself, so that God thereby does evil, but towards the good that follows from it, the manifestations of his justice and above all of his mercy. That God's will does not itself lead to evil is brought out by James when he writes: 'Let no one say when he is tempted, "I am tempted by God"; for God cannot be tempted with evil and he himself tempts no one; but each person is tempted when he is lured and enticed by his own desire' (James 1: 13–14). This statement and the one which speaks of God's patience in suffering our sins formed the idea of 'permission' which is the one most employed in theological and ecclesiastical usage today. It expresses a correction of the old biblical manner of speaking, according to which God himself hardens the heart of Pharaoh and would thus seem to will and cause sin. But even the idea of permission must in its turn be corrected on the basis of this biblical style of language: all inability and ignorance, which are so often the source of human permission, must here be denied. We have already said that this permission is a moment within the whole activity of God, in the same way as the creation of the spiritual soul. But between the particularity of each of these moments there exists a contrast. As such, the creation of the soul escapes the activity of human beings, but the permission of evil does not fall outside the activity of God. Here we once more experience a shortage of words and ideas. Let us therefore satisfy ourselves with this conclusion: God, who created man for heaven, so makes him to be a free person that he even realises him in his own turning away into sin and hell.

Thus we have completed our treatment of the three points in this section. We have considered God's creation in itself, in comparison with his maintenance, moving and government, and in comparison with the activity of the creature itself. We hope thus to have fulfilled the wish that we expressed at the beginning of this section, namely that everything should remain in the religious context which the sources of revelation have always kept alive. Now, however, we should like in a final survey to make the religious value of the faith in creation, such as we have expounded it in this section, more clearly experienced. In doing this we do not need to repeat what has been said in the preceding section, only to extend it a little.

We have already referred to the majesty of God in his creation and the source of praise that arises out of it, above all in the psalms. Let us add to this that throughout the world dependence on God must find expression in his service. This may briefly be related to two ideas from the first section of our earlier chapter, that of holiness and that of the covenant. In connection with the latter idea we may repeat what has already been said: that God offers his covenant and so summons men to love, but that at the same time a requirement is contained therein. It is a covenant in adoration and a love in service, because the creation relationship persists in its entirety in the covenant, and any denial of it would make the covenant with the living God empty and useless for man. This point may nevertheless be left, since we shall go more closely into the relation between creation and covenant in the next chapter.

A word or two more about holiness; not that of God, but that of his creature. It consists primarily in the separating of someone or something for the worship of God. This takes place, however, whilst the whole 'earth is Yahweh's and the fullness thereof, the world and those who dwell therein' (Ps 24 (23): 1). Yahweh himself also expressly declares this when he consecrates Israel to himself (Ex 19:5). In the holiness of the cult, therefore, we see visibly and manifestly expressed with respect to certain things that which is anchored in the deepest being of all things, namely their belonging to God. Thus not only the holy, but equally the profane, is of God and for his glory. This is most important, because we sinful human beings are always trying to avoid God's demands by entrenching ourselves in the profane and at the same time acknowledging him that much more, as if camouflaged in the holy. We do not suggest, over and against this, that the distinction between holy and profane must be abolished, thus that the profane should be sacralised or taken over by the church, but that it is completely taken up in the service of the creator, of which the cultic, the holy is the most direct expression.

All of the above concerns the complete dependence of the creature with respect to the creator. But it is just as much part of the religious attitude which arises from belief in the creation that we should look at the matter from the opposite direction and wholly accept that God himself realises and wills the reality and individuality of the creature. There is thus a religious and christian humanism which finds its roots in faith in the creation and especially in faith in the incarnation. It is not expressly confessed in ecclesiastical pronouncements about the creation, but it is clearly present in all sorts of attitudes and decisions of the church, and is even one of the characteristics of our catholic faith as opposed to that of the reformation. The expression of faith concerning the accessibility of God's existence to our natural reason, which we have already met in our first chapter, is a first expression of it. The fact that in the practical use of that reason a revelation is necessary for the knowledge of God and of divine matters does not contradict this first pronouncement, since it is concerned only with the capabilities, the structure, the nature of the human being, not with the free use which he makes of these. What the church is here affirming against fideism and what she has constantly affirmed against the reformation is that sin turns our capacities and being away from God, but does not destroy any part of them. God's creative power remains unassailable by sin and even by original sin, even though the latter reaches to the deepest roots of our being. This creation by God does not maintain a neutral zone within the creature, it maintains the being of the creature within the denial of sin, which weighs upon the whole of created reality.

Even in its sinfulness, therefore, this being is addressed and called upon by God's grace. It also carries within it laws which hold as much for the sinful man as for the one accepting grace. Hence also the specifically catholic appeal to the laws of nature, an appeal which is essential to our faith, although the moralists who maintain it will do well to remember that here also revelation is sometimes needed to free the reason for insight into the actual nature of man and that this nature is always present in a form modified by a particular culture. Catholic theology and practice have rightly maintained the individuality of the creature against all one-sided views of grace or sin. In our days, however, they must maintain it against a tendency to make the creature disappear before God in prayer and mysticism, or rather, in faulty expressions of these. It is wrong, for example, when the veneration of saints is no problem because God is placed on their level; but neither may it become problematic or even objectionable because God's all-surpassing reality might be thought to annihilate or swallow up all creaturely existence which is not directly accessible to our sense. In fact, not only the role of the saints, but also and above all that of Christ's humanity in the heavenly existence has found too small a place in various theological considerations. Similarly, perhaps, in some theological accounts of authentic christian mysticism which include the contrasting relation God-creature under the platonic formula 'all-nothing'.

Yet not only within the holy itself, but above all in the profane sphere, there is an urgent need to emphasise the existence—and thus the right to existence—and the individuality and individual value of the creature. It is precisely the baptising of the profane that demands first and foremost the acknowledgement of that same profane reality. This intrinsic value was accentuated in the renaissance, often accentuated over and against God, but the balance will only be restored when on God's account, i.e., by virtue of our faith in creation, we fully acknowledge the value of the profane. In modern man there is a need, brought about because he does not feel that acknowledgement to be present in religion.

Thus our faith in creation is the source for a religious and humanitarian attitude; thus it already provides us with an apostolic task.[1] As far as earthly realities are concerned this faith in creation must certainly be proclaimed with a true spirit of christian equilibrium. For it is proper to 'the prince of this world' to hide his dependence on the creator by an over-emphasis of the very real value of created reality and to suppress the holy by continually increasing solicitude for the profane. It cannot be denied that in our contemporary culture his design is to a great extent succeeding. Christ, in contrast, redeems us by his detachment and cross. But he redeems us into life, into the new heaven and the new earth, to which the whole of creation in some way returns, and certainly the whole man, with soul and body. We may therefore on the one hand not forget detachment and cross, but must on the other be on our guard against movements which might threaten to identify evil with a particular domain of reality: earthly reality, the body, sexuality. Detachment and cross are much more the way to acceptance of all creation, but then on the basis of the creator, who is at the same time Father, and in Christ Jesus. But now we are well into the doctrine of the redemption. Let it be enough for us to have finished, at least for the present, the doctrine of creation.

[1] On this last point, see: Karl Rahner, 'Die ewige Bedeutung der Menschheit Jesu für unser Gottesverhältnis', *Geist und Leben* 26 (1953), 279–88; R. Guardini, *The World and the Person*, Chicago 1965.

3
Nature and grace

In the preceding chapters we have followed the order of the history of revelation in speaking about God as the covenant-God—and thus already in some degree as Father—and as creator. We have already pointed out that one may rightly deal with these considerations in the reverse order, not only on account of apologetical motives, but also by virtue of the arrangement in which the book of Genesis, and with it the whole bible, has finally come down to us. This order allows us to survey the whole of God's plan of salvation from the beginning and enables us in addition to make manifest the essence of God's covenant and of the gifts given thereby. This latter is the reason why we shall now, in our third chapter, sketch the special nature of God's covenant and covenant-gifts against the background of the creation. Here we shall talk about a distinction which theology and ecclesiastical authority make emphatically. It is referred to by the terms 'nature' and 'grace', which, for this reason, we have chosen as the title for this chapter, in which we shall approach the distinction between these two realities on the basis of what has been said in our earlier chapters concerning covenant and creation; not yet on the basis of Christ and his work, for these only come under discussion with the second article of faith.

Creation and covenant

As we have just noted, not only theology, but also the teaching authority of the church has distinguished, in a real way, God's giving of grace from what man has and is as creature, and from what every creature has and is precisely as creature; in brief, from the nature of the creature. First and foremost that teaching authority proclaims, in accordance with the whole of tradition and with scripture itself, that God's gifts of grace are completely above and beyond the rights and powers of the sinful human race, fallen in Adam. For the moment, however, we wish to leave this and concern ourselves with the transcendence of these gifts of grace with respect to man and creature as such, with respect to created nature. That is, we wish to occupy ourselves with what theologians term the completely supernatural character of gifts of grace. The theologians affirm this completely supernatural character in the most thorough way with regard to the most central gifts, namely sanctifying grace and the infused virtues of faith, hope, and love connected with it; their teaching goes back to the idea of the divinisation of man, which is found among the Greek fathers of the church. But the teaching authority of the church has also pronounced in favour of this absolutely supernatural character. By their respective condemnation of the propositions of Baius and Quesnel, Popes Pius v and Clement xi made it clear that even for the first human beings in their innocence, grace was not theirs by right (Dz 1021, 1023, 1385). The First Vatican Council contrasts faith with natural reason as being supernatural through its principle and its object, and names as the object of that faith: 'the mysteries hidden in God which cannot be known without revelation from God' (Dz 1795, 1816). In his letter *Gravissimas inter,* Pope Pius XI says that they 'surpass not only human philosophy, but also the natural understanding of the angels' (Dz 1675). So that one can say in general that the ordinary teaching authority of the church preaches the completely supernatural character of the gifts of grace.

When we now seek this supernatural character in scripture, it seems at first not to be found. Nowhere does scripture speak of the granting of grace to angels; if anything at all is said about a separate giving of grace as far as the first human beings before the fall are concerned, then it is said in a heavily veiled way. For the rest, the humanity that is given grace is always the fallen humanity. Nevertheless, the absolutely supernatural character of the gifts of grace can be discerned from scriptural data in another way, namely from the structure of these gifts themselves. In the New Testament we find them connected with the Holy Spirit and with the Father and Son, as gifts of childhood. Since we are restricting ourselves in these chapters to the first article of faith, we shall not go any further into this at present. But the gifts of grace are also found in connection with the covenant between God and his people. We have already pointed out that the Hebrew word for grace, *hesed,* indicates a service or favour which takes place in a covenant. And it is also true that as one investigates in further detail the supernatural, unearned nature attributed to grace, one is directed towards the biblical idea of 'covenant'. For this supernatural and unearned nature is expressed by saying that God is completely free to give these gifts, that he can also withhold them. This freedom, however, is also that of God's act of creation, as we have already shown in the previous chapter. The concepts 'unearned' and 'gift', however, say something which distinguishes God's freedom in giving grace from his freedom in creating. For here there is reference to freedom with respect to an existing person, which is precisely what is completely lacking in the case of creation. Creation and the giving of grace are thus one as far as God's perfect freedom is concerned, but differ in that the freedom of creation presupposes nothing and no one; indeed, it precisely excludes the supposition of anything or anyone outside God, whilst it is proper to the freedom of giving grace that it supposes something, or rather someone, apart from God. This is the granting of grace to someone, an unearned gift to someone, and so this presupposition is implicit in its freedom. The freedom of creation is a freedom pure and simple, in a vacuum one might say, but the freedom of giving grace is freedom with regard to a person, a partner. It will be seen that this is precisely the freedom of God's covenant, because this also presupposes persons outside him as partners.

We might now work this out in more detail by showing how the gifts of grace are all gifts of the covenant. But this is not the place to demonstrate the supernatural character of sanctifying grace, and the rest—that must come in the discussion of further articles of faith. Here we have tried only to elaborate in some detail the distinction between covenant and creation and so also the unearned nature of the former, so as later to build upon this foundation in making clear the supernatural character of the grace of the New Testament. Just as in the second section of the previous chapter we gave ample attention to the creation, so we shall now work out the nature of the covenant in its distinction from and co-existence with the creation. In order to consider creation we proceeded from the various forms of human making, and saw this realised without imperfections and thus in a higher, in fact completely different manner in God. When we now come to discuss God's covenant against the background of his creation, we shall see the human activities which bring about or experience a covenant against the background of making in general by man, and we shall in the same way ascend from this complex to God. Thus, first something concerning human covenant-activity in its contrast and connection with human making, then concerning God's covenant-activity in its contrast and connection with his creation.

Covenant-activity among human beings

When in the preceding chapter we considered human production, we mainly emphasised its imperfection. Yet in the first instance it possesses a perfection. Making is the highest expression of the 'dominion' for which man has been created in God's image (Gen 1 : 26), and in its highest forms we refer to this human making with the same word as divine making, namely 'creation'. Work, craft, expression, art, all this is the expression of a dominion over material things, even including one's own body. Man stands as subject before an object, a something, something of a lower order, and this justifies the attitude of dominance. This attitude is the same when it comes to investigation and research, and it is also justified there, although it is just the most brilliant specialist, like the most competent technologist, who will in the difficulties of his work also have to acknowledge the limits of his dominion. But a man's attitude must become something completely different when he stands before another human subject, a someone; when a person meets another person. Even here a person can stick obstinately to the attitude of ruling something and thereby suppress the personal encounter, as in slavery and other forms of exploitation. But the human conscience—especially when it has been restored in its humanity by christianity—clearly sees a sin in this, a sin that even cries out for vengeance. The attitude required towards another person is one that is based on the recognition of an equal, it is one of respect and distance, above all of the respect of freedom; of a co-existence on the basis of equality, but even more so, one of mutual approach in free self-revelation, in mutual giving and gratitude, in short: in love. Love must be present in some way in every encounter between persons, and it will always bring about something of a covenant.

Here we perceive the most fundamental difference between the two forms of human activity which we named: on the one side making, on the other meeting, entering into covenant, the activity of subject-subject relationships, or intersubjectivity. The difference lies in the radical dissimilarity between the 'other party' in these relations and in its respective recognition by a different basic attitude in the interaction; it is the difference between the attitude of love and that of dominance. In fact everything has been said about these two forms of human activity when this basic difference of attitude has been shown, since for the rest they are the same. For in both activity takes place over and against a reaction and in both the same human capacities for action are brought into play. This similarity must not be isolated from the difference, however, for the difference is once more manifested in the aspects of similarity mentioned. Let us look into this somewhat more closely.

Whenever man acts there is always action and reaction, but in the making of something this interplay varies very much from that in meeting someone. The reaction of the thing, and also of the material character of the other by virtue of his physical nature (for instance, the reaction in a fight, a surgical operation or a psychic influence), is calculated and then used, eliminated or overcome, in one word: the person acting tries to govern this reaction. However, the other person's reaction arises out of his freedom and must therefore be received in freedom. Here no investigation, but faith; no calculation, but trust; no utilisation, but love; no domination, but encounter. Of course, the fact must not be concealed that in the encounter, disbelief, mistrust, and hatred can also arise (which, moreover, hinders the encounter itself). But even when this happens there remains a recognition of the person, because things are not treated with disbelief, mistrust or hatred. Not only are a person's actions and disposition with regard to possible reaction differently ordered according to whether he is faced with a thing or with a person, but in the latter case they are expressly orientated towards a reaction or proceed expressly from one. For in the contact between human being and thing action is always accompanied by reaction, but there is no intention of exchange on the same level. This, however, is always aimed at in intersubjective activity, as an exchange that is free from both sides, as a dialogue. Human intersubjectivity or interpersonal activity is meaningful and directed from both sides, and it takes place through the body and the world of things. That is why the body takes part not only as sensory receptor or instrument, but also as expression. Man always achieves his intersubjective contact in symbolic activity, of which language is the highest form.

And so we come to the discussion of capacities which are realised in this contact. For, just as the relation between action and reaction has, as we have just said, a different structure in intersubjectivity from that in subject-object relationships, so also the relation between the various operations of human capacities. In the symbolic character of interpersonal activity there appears a greater unity—to put it more accurately: a more intimate mutual penetration of mental and sensory action. Here the spirit does not take the distance that is taken in generalisation, calculation and the formulation of laws, but continually approaches the other person from a different side so as to discover a total view composed of various aspects; and in approaching it also expresses its own individuality in signs. In this the intuitive character of the spirit penetrates more into the senses, something which is seen in the forms of aesthetic intuition, erotic intuition, and between these, in the different forms of face-to-face expression: as much in the loving or admiring gaze as in the averted look. Verbs which are used to express a feeling point at the same time to a co-operation between intellect and will (and equally between sensory perception and love or hostility). In all the forms of knowing the will is active in bringing into operation or restraining the various perceptual capacities: knowledge of persons, however, is the receiving and giving of what faith, hope and love, or disbelief, mistrust and hate bring with them and that not just as final result, but as a continual influence upon the process of the very knowledge out of which they arise. A much more detailed discussion of all this could be given, but we have mentioned it only in order to provide as starting-point for the consideration of God's activity a concrete view of the most fundamental contrast within human activity, at least when that consists in going outwards: the contrast between subject-object activity and intersubjective activity.

But here there is not only contrast, but also coincidence. For we human beings meet each other within a world of things, and always draw these into our encounter, if only in such a subtle form as the making of air vibrations in speaking. In addition to this, however, we have a body, and on this earth it is partly a thing and an object for others and in some degree also for ourselves. (It is just in this measure that we *have* a body and yet *are* not that body.) This is why one's approach to a person is always accompanied by the making and achieving of something. But conversely, orientation towards someone is also always present in some measure in all our making, whether as starting-point or as final aim. This is quite clear in our inward activity, namely in our thought, which always forms words, which is always inward expression. But our external activity with things can also always be connected with interpersonal contact; it takes place by virtue of teaching or instruction, it is itself the production of expressions, it is accomplished for the benefit of or out of love for another or others; yes, all construction of the world comes about through us human beings, and this not by each one of us separately, but in continual exchange.

So the two forms of activity which we sketched, subject-object and intersubjective activity, are nowhere found alone. We have thus not described two separate forms, but rather two elements which are present in every outwardly directed activity of man, although always in different proportions. So if we were to survey human activities as they in fact occur, we should be able to perceive a scale among them, on which positions depend on the degree to which the interpersonal aspect is represented in an activity. Roughly speaking, one can distinguish three groups of activities. Firstly work, including technical work, in which interpersonal contact only determines the separate activity from without, namely in so far as it takes place according to the teaching, plan, or instruction of another person, or for another's use. Secondly, work which brings about a particular expression, artistically or not, thus work in which the interpersonal contact is not an external starting-point or destination, but inwardly determines the structure and result of the activity, for instance, in the making of an image of some sort, or the writing of a letter. Thirdly and finally, activities in which the making and achievement are completely and wholly taken up in the expression and are so permeated by it that they have no real existence of their own, as is primarily the case with speech and also with the 'language' of music, dance, gesture, love-making, and so on. This division also admits many intermediate cases: trade, communication techniques, and so on.

Nor is it the only possible division. One could also, for example, divide according to the degree in which the interpersonal aspect dominates the relations which arise between human beings. That is to say, it can be the case that I have already distinguished the other person from the thing, and respect him, but only in his rights; that I feel myself bound with regard to his rights, but know him on the other hand to be bound by my rights. For in this sphere of law the acknowledgement of the person is present and active in the background—since no rights are granted to things—but he is only regarded in a general way as 'a human being', not in his irreplaceable individuality. That is why what law characterises is not what a person is, but what he has—'to everyone his due'—and what he achieves in exchange for an equivalent achievement—*do ut des*. Legal order is a system of balance between rights and duties. But it is surpassed by the meeting between persons as such and the community which arises thereby. This is the sphere of free, unearned giving, of humble and grateful acceptance, of the self-manifestation and faith, the support and trust, the love and love in return which cannot be forced (in fact, ultimately also of the negation of all this, because hatred of someone can go together with a strict respect of his rights and is, even if negative, an estimation of value that surpasses the recognition of rights).

This division between the orders of law and love corresponds to some extent with the one we made above in human activities according to the greater or less element of interpersonality in an activity. For in so far as it relates, as such, to another person, and so occurs for the use and benefit of someone else, it is precisely the making of something that forms the content of rights and duties; it is an achievement which demands another achievement in return. Not only can expression as such, especially artistic expression and above all that of love not be forced, it can neither be ordered nor repaid. Yet the continuity which we pointed out in our first division of human activity also holds between the spheres of law and love. For in the first place, no legal system can last without an authentic recognition of persons as its background—one thinks, for example, of the humanisation of industrial relations—or without strict equality always being accompanied by 'fairness': *summum ius summa iniuria*! For our purpose, however, it is more important to realise that relations of love are also incarnated in a legal system, and at the same time surpass it: thus is the case, for instance, with marriage and family. We believe this to be important because it is just in this that God's covenant activity surpasses that of human beings in a radical way. That is why it is now time to talk about this divine activity.

God's covenant-activity

The most important data concerning the fact that God stands in a covenant relation to 'his people' (Israel and Christ's church) have already been discussed in the first section of our first chapter. And this is a fact, certainly as regards the Old Covenant. But the New Testament is also a covenant. It is true that in the sacred books of the New Testament the covenant terminology recedes to the background and in tradition ideas such as God's descent and man's exaltation in Christ, as also those of our being made children of God and incorporated in his Son, have very much received precedence over the more general idea of the covenant; yet nevertheless, the latter is and remains active in the background. We again find its influence above all when the attitude of the man of the New Testament is more closely defined. Here, more than under the old dispensation, this is referred to in definite terms. It is first and foremost 'faith'—that word which the christians ultimately used to refer to the whole of their religion —also 'hope' and finally 'love', love for human beings, but also for God. 'Faith, hope, love, these three' (1 Cor 13: 13), are man's answer in the covenant into which God enters with him in Christ (and, in fact, much more than a human answer). Thus the New Testament is just as much and even more deeply 'covenant' than the Old, and we see that it refers back past the Mosaic covenant to that made by God with Abraham as if to a common origin (Gal 4: 22–31; Rm 4; Heb 11: 19). When we now survey this single covenant in its old and new phases, whose unity as covenant is symbolised in Abraham and whose difference and contrast is expressed in the mediators Moses and Christ—when we thus survey this covenant between God and man, we once more discover, more sublimely expressed, the perfections of interpersonal activity among human beings.

We see then that God's covenant-activity surpasses man's intersubjective activity as much as his creative activity surpasses man's subject-object activity. God's creation is a making by him alone, without supposing anything or anyone, while on the other hand the whole reality of the creature is dependent upon him. In his creation God is completely free and completely and utterly the origin. This majesty of divine creation, which we attempted to describe in the second section of the preceding chapter, is found once more in his covenant-activity. Here also he is completely free, and completely and utterly origin. Not by presupposing nothing or no one, for the covenant with man precisely presupposes man; but man in his turn is God's creature and so God presupposes nothing apart from himself, only his own creation. On the other hand, this presupposition of man by God is a very serious matter, because God asks of him a free acceptance at every instant and thereby continually allows him the possibility of a free refusal (in so far as man himself has not established his choice for eternity). But we must turn our attention back to God and say that just as the creature with the whole of its reality is from God, so also all that the covenant gives to the creature is from God, God's completely free gift, including even the free reply of the creature. Here the mystery of the coincidence of God's total causality and man's freedom returns on a higher level. It may also be expressed thus: in both creation and covenant the dilemma 'God or man' is excluded, in both God alone is the cause of man's being himself; in creation it is God's command alone that causes man to freely realise himself, in the covenant it is again solely God's calling that enables man to answer freely.

The rough outlines we have set down as a comparison between creation and covenant may be seen in concrete form when one looks over the history of the Old and New Testaments. In the Old Testament it is especially noticeable how in the making of the covenant the initiative lies completely with God. For Abraham life in covenant with Yahweh is begun by a call, in fact a command, to depart from his land, a command which is immediately accompanied by God's promises (Gen 12: 1–3). In Genesis 17 this covenant is described in more detail, as also, with strong emphasis upon God's promises, in Genesis 22 after the sacrifice Abraham was ready to make of his only son. Something is also asked of Abraham himself, namely circumcision (Gen 17: 10–14), but even more that he should 'walk before me, and be blameless' (Gen 17: 1). However, this walking before the face of Yahweh primarily signifies the recognition of God as Abraham's refuge in all things. Several events in the Genesis story of Abraham—and even more so in the life of Jacob—appear at first sight only as picturesque or even piquant illustrations, but on closer inspection they reveal to us the lessons these patriarchs had to go through in order to look in all matters to God's care and wisdom for their salvation, and not to search for it in their own astuteness. It is above all as regards God's central promise, that of descendents and a land, that Abraham is a man of faith and hope, and therefore pleasing to God: 'He believed Yahweh;

and he reckoned it to him as righteousness' (Gen 15:6).

The above details from the history of Abraham are representative of all the further history of the covenant, both of that established in Moses and of the new and eternal covenant in Christ. The initiative is always with God. This is clearly seen in the vocation and sending forth of Moses once he seeks strength only in Yahweh's might, his own attempts having failed. The exodus and the journey in the desert are also due to Yahweh's power and initiative; here God not only makes Israel his own people, he even makes them a people as such, and punishes those who grumble and show their lack of faith, including Moses. The stories of the Judges and of David speak the same language, for it is precisely on account of his faith and devotion that David, rather than Saul, is the man dear to Yahweh. The organisation of the people of the covenant through law, public worship, and theocratic kingship threatens to push into the background the attitude necessary for the people of the covenant, but the prophets preach it more than any other commandment. Here we only need to recall the prophets' struggle for personal consecration to Yahweh against a purely ritual holiness, in other words, for a complete giving up of man's 'heart' to the freedom of God. It is above all during the Babylonian crisis that God's freedom is made visible in events and expressed in the words of the prophets. Yahweh can chastise and abandon his people, and he will do so; such is the message of Jeremiah. And Ezekiel, who sees a new beginning of contact with God opening among the exiles, is the most firm in emphasising that the initiative in the covenant lay from the beginning with Yahweh's loving kindness and at the end with his mercy: this above all in his chapter on Jerusalem as a foundling and a harlot (Ez 16). In this way the prophets are the first to lay a strong and polemical emphasis on the proclamation of Yahweh's freedom, which we have already seen so clearly in the ancient stories.

It is on the basis of this prophetic doctrine of grace that the truly chosen members of Israel's remnant, 'the poor of Yahweh' live, while in the other direction Israel's heroic struggle for God's law under the Macchabees also leads to a mystification of this people in pharisaism. Opposed to the latter we find a second great proclamation of God's freedom with the advent of the New Testament. Now Israel undergoes a crisis: whether to cling fast to its ancient institutions, above all to its law, in order to defend itself against the kingdom of God which is breaking into its history in God's Son, or to be converted and believe. In the face of the disbelief with which he meets, Jesus emphasises most strongly that it is only the Father who according to his own pleasure reveals him to 'babes' (see for example, Mt 11:25f.=Lk 10:21; Mt 16:17; Jn 3:13, 6:37–39, 44f., 65; 8:42f., 47; 10:26). Over and against this, man must give his obedience to the Father's will (Mt 6:10; 7:21; Mk 3:35=Mt 12:50=Lk 8:21; Lk 11:28), he must fulfil the first and greatest commandment by loving God with the whole of his being (Mt 22:37=Lk 10:27), he must believe and, as the beginning of all this, repent (Mk 1:15=Mt 4:17). The same attitudes in God and man are also preached by the apostles. One could point to references in their writings to God's freedom, his foreknowledge, his predestination (see, for example: Rm 8:29f.; Eph 1:4f.; Phil 1:6; Col 1:13; Jas 1:18; 1 Jn 4:10), and we have already spoken about the human reply of faith and hope. This is brought out even more clearly than in Jesus' preaching through the fact that rejection of the Pharisees' position is developed, particularly by

Paul, in terms of a viewpoint which is contrasted with that of the Old Testament (i.e., the Old Testament, it must be noted, to which the Jew clings to the exclusion of the New). It occurs primarily through an even stronger emphasis on the aspect of God's freedom in certain Old Testament ideas than the prophets had already given. We have pointed out that in the word 'grace' its character of being unearned, its aspect of favour, will come over more strongly than its being a gift within a mutual covenant. Thus the New Testament words *charis* and *eleos* are filled with the idea of God's mercy towards the sinful human being, thus of God's free initiative, more than the Hebrew word *hesed*. Such is also the case with the word that is used for the covenant itself. For this the writers of the gospels and letters use the Greek translation of the Hebrew *berith* already provided by the Septuagint, namely *diathēkē*. This word primarily signifies 'testament' and thus the Vulgate, in imitation of the Septuagint, also uses the word *testamentum* rather than *foedus* in the New Testament books. However, *testamentum* means the declaration of one's will, and thereby strongly emphasises that the initiative proceeds from God—and Christ. We cannot point to an explicit reflection upon this meaning anywhere in the New Testament books, for on the only occasion when the idea of 'testament' is analysed it is connected with 'the death of the testator' (Heb 9: 16). Even there it appears that the initiative proceeds in the first place from God, that here God defines his institutions. However, this does not exclude the idea of covenant. Perhaps because even a human testament constitutes a relationship between persons and only has effect through its acceptance by the inheritor; but certainly because in the books of the New Testament it is made sufficiently clear, on the other hand, that God also 'calls' and thereby gives man the opportunity to reply (cf God's disposition and calling as regards Christ and his reply in Heb 5: 1–6 and 10: 5–9; with Mary: Lk 1: 31–36, 38). In this way the human reply is included, but the emphasis is primarily on God's freedom.

However, this is not only implicit in the vocabulary of the New Testament writers, it is explicitly revealed in their view of the history of the Old Testament. Here mention must be given in the first place to Stephen's address in Acts 7. Its principle theme is expressed in the sentence, 'You always resist the Holy Spirit. As your fathers did, so do you' (Acts 7: 51). This resistance, which ended, in fact, with the murder of Jesus, is an adherence to institutions over and against the freedom of God, an adherence to temple, cult, and law. But the realities to which the Jews cling are empty when they are set in opposition to God, because 'the Most High does not dwell in houses made with hand' (Acts 7: 48), and the law 'delivered by angels' is not kept (7: 53). In contrast with this attitude of the Jews there stands that of their fathers, Abraham and Moses, which is described at the beginning of Stephen's address, in imitation of Jesus' own appeal to these two. Now all these thoughts from the first martyr's address are to be found once more in the theology of St Paul. For him also the old dispensation consists of 'weak and beggarly elements' (Gal 4: 9), and this is developed as regards the whole of the cult in the letter to the Hebrews, as regards the law in the letter to the Romans, and as regards law and circumcision in the letter to the Galatians. Thus one does God's work of salvation in the cross of Christ an injustice if one pronounces circumcision and the works of the law necessary for justification (Gal 2: 14–21; 5: 1–5 and passim). It is not the 'works of the law', the achievement of keeping God's commands—which in any case is carried out neither by Paul nor by the Jews—that makes man righteous, but faith, which is self-giving and adherence to Christ, and that alone. The relationship between God as legislator and man as the one who fulfils the legislation (in reality or in the imagination) is not ideal, and man does wrong in wishing to install himself in such a relationship. This relationship is not even the original one, which is why the three letters mentioned refer back past the mosaic covenant to that made with Abraham, with its dialogue between promise and faith. More so than in its institutional elaboration in the mosaic version, this original covenant has been brought to completion in the new and eternal covenant in Christ Jesus. Now God has fulfilled his promises and a man must manifest himself as the seed of Abraham by giving himself in faith to that fulfilment. Let this brief presentation suffice as a conclusion to the whole teaching of scripture on God's freedom in his covenant, a freedom by which he surpasses covenant activity among men in the same degree that his creation surpasses human making.

This freedom-in-covenant has ultimately been translated in theological and ecclesiastical usage by the notion of 'supernatural'. In this the covenant relation has been very much pushed into the background. At the beginning of this chapter, however, we have already attempted to make this background visible once more, to show that one is justified in seeking the roots of a doctrine of the completely supernatural character of grace in that of the covenant. Now we may show in a more exact way how both of these contrasts, that between creation and covenant and that between nature and supernatural gift, express the same reality, how both pairs of ideas may be translated in terms of each other.

As we have already said, the supernatural—more accurately, the completely supernatural, that which is supernatural with respect to each and every creature—is defined as that which surpasses the powers and demands of the creature. We have also already shown, at the beginning of this section, that this definition can be reduced to that which God gives in his covenant with his creatures. Having developed in more detail the idea of the covenant with God, however, we should now like to show that the idea of the supernatural means precisely the same as the freedom of God in that covenant. We have already made it clear that the supernatural presupposes someone for whom it is what it is, supernatural; now let us demonstrate that 'the supernatural' is the direct translation of the way in which God's covenant surpasses all human encounters.

This is true first of all in the fact that it surpasses the *powers* of the creature. Every contact between human persons as such, with all the exchange of inward and outward gifts, implies that what one contributes surpasses the capacities of the other. We must express this in more detail, however. Here we wish to speak in the first place about the powers of the man who receives in regard to the giver, the capacities for outward action through which something is withdrawn from the person who gives; not the powers of internal assimilation, of immanent action by which one makes what is given one's own. On the one hand, we human beings have in our body the only means of interpersonal contact, while on the other during this mortal life we continually experience this body as an obstacle to our personal existence, as a thing. For this last reason I can always in some way achieve and even force an approach to the other, I can to some extent read his interior from what his body manifests, from his behaviour towards people other than myself, from unconscious bodily manifestations such as blushing, or from the consideration of artefacts such as handwriting; in fact, I can force the other person's body into service, into presence, even into the action which in marriage is the sign of the deepest union. But from this it now also becomes clear that the actual personal being of the other cannot be manipulated by me; it cannot be investigated, traced or laid hold of, but must be revealed by him and believed by me; it cannot be forced, but must be promised or given by him and accepted by me in trust and gratitude. Thus there is a boundary between that which I can obtain from another person by my own powers and that which lies outside or above my powers and can only be given by the other person in freedom. Approach to the other lies, in so far as he does not express himself as a person, inside my power, but in so far as he does, beyond it. But it is only in theory that this boundary can be sharply drawn. In practice it does not remain fixed, because with the same body someone may express himself as a person for one man and not for another, in fact in the same body one has expressions which are subject to personal freedom and those which stand outside it, together in indivisible unity. What one person is to another certainly belongs to a sphere of secrecy between those two, but through our bodiliness it is often accessible under many aspects to a third party. Indeed, what another personally reveals to me can enable me to penetrate to that which he wishes to keep secret. Thus from an abstract point of view personal communication between human beings certainly surpasses the powers of the one who receives it, but seeing that no single human being, and in this case the one who is communicating, ever fully realises himself as a person in this life, this personal communication from another never lies purely above the powers of whoever is receiving it.

With God, however, this precisely is the case. God with his holiness therefore excludes all magic, as we have already shown. His covenant is a purely personal communication and its gifts are in no way whatsoever attainable or coercible by our powers. All that we have just said about the difficulty of drawing a line separating man as a person from man as a thing must be completely omitted in the case of God. Another human person always surpasses our powers in his personal self-communication, but not completely; only God does so completely and utterly.

One might complete this first half of the definition of the supernatural by saying that only God gives a pure revelation. I can sometimes anticipate the personal revelation of another human being by my conclusions from his behaviour or by penetrating the sphere existing between him and a third person; through my knowledge of human beings I can also see into and interpret that self-revelation, perhaps even better than the man who is doing the revealing can fathom himself out (the intuition of the educator and spiritual adviser). But we can in no way anticipate God's revelation, it is pure surprise; yes, something new to the knowledge which we have of him through our natural capacities (knowledge we do not acquire, moreover, by exercising our powers upon him, but upon his creatures; while in the conclusion from this to God's existence there still lies a free handing over of oneself). Moreover, given God's revelation, we cannot simply make it the point of departure for conclusions as if it was the actual object of our rational knowledge (cf Dz 1796), but theologising is always, and most fully in the development of the church's understanding of her faith, a listening.

The supernatural surpasses not only the powers of the creature, but thereby also his *demands*, his rights, that which he merits. This is less difficult to translate into terms of interpersonality than what has gone before. For we are inclined to connect the powers with nature; but that which surpasses demands, rights, or merit is unearned, *gratuitum*, freely given, gift; and all these words already refer more clearly to the person, in fact they point to interpersonal communication in so far as it surpasses the legal sphere. Yet this sphere of law is itself already an initial and incomplete form of interpersonal relations, as we pointed out above. We also pointed out there in passing that even the relations of the most personal love between human beings, for example, in marriage and family, are incarnated in a legal order, and that God's covenant-activity radically surpasses that of man on this point. Thus here we have the same situation as above, where we spoke about the surpassing of the individual's power. The self-communication of the human person transcends the powers of the person receiving it, but not completely. Such is also the case with laws and rights. Here again the border between the spheres of law and love may only be precisely drawn in the abstract, while in the concrete even the most personal relations of love are always partly defined by laws. The expression of love in a fleeting encounter is almost completely outside the legal sphere, but its fleeting character makes it rather a case of amorousness than of love. When love goes deeper it also becomes more total, in time also. And thus already friendship has its unwritten rights and duties. But precisely the deepest and most human love under all aspects, that between man and woman, also creates marriage as a legal institution; and the love between parents and children, which is an extension of marital love, knows rights and duties in its turn. These exist in the normal exchange of love only in being surpassed, but they make themselves obvious as soon as love falls away from its most personal realisation and in the most extreme cases they may even be enforced by higher legal authority. From this it is clear why this incarnation in a legal system is necessary on earth for interpersonal life. For man is not personalised in the whole of his being. We have just shown above how with their powers others can penetrate via a human being's physical aspect into his own personality; now we must note that it is also possible for anyone to become removed from his own personality in his relations with others. He can fail to make the vital sphere an expression and vehicle, and instead set it up as independent, thus neglecting, misusing, or betraying personal relations. He is protected against this by the fact that the bond of love is also juridically fixed. Thus from the possibility of this falling from pure interpersonality and from the fact that in this earthly life we are not yet fully personalised in the whole of our being, it follows necessarily that the spheres of love and law are in practice mixed.

Now this is just the point regarding which God's covenant surpasses human ties. His gifts do not fall under the sphere of law and therefore transcend not only the powers but also the demands of the creature. The latter is always more difficult to accept than the former. It would certainly seem as if man, when he experiences God's grace as something beyond his powers, nevertheless still wishes to 'stick to his rights'. This he did during the Old Testament, and that is why we heard the prophets and Stephen speaking out against self-exaltation in worship, and Paul against boasting about fulfilment of the law. It is not by virtue of all these works that man becomes righteous before God and a child of his, but through God's pure gift. In the church of the New Testament it was proclaimed against jansenism that even the undefiled nature of the first human beings before their sin contained within it not a single right to God's gifts, in particular to eternal life. It is especially these pronouncements, which we had already mentioned, that constitute the reason for including the surpassing of the creature's rights in the definition of the supernatural.

In the same way that we express the transcendence of created powers positively by saying that in his covenant God purely reveals, so now we might present the surpassing of all the creature's rights by saying God purely and simply gives. The gift of the covenant is pure gift and the word 'grace' brings this character clearly into our mind. What we said concerning marriage makes it clear that there the most intimate devotion, the deepest form of giving nevertheless continues to retain the aspect of 'what is due', the *debitum* of pauline terminology (1 Cor 7:3) which the moralists took over. Indeed, love always expresses itself in a giving to which someone may claim a right and in the fulfilling of laws, so that again Paul can say: 'Owe no one anything, except to love one another; for he who loves his neighbour has fulfilled the law' (Rm 13:8). God, however, granted gifts which are completely and utterly beyond our rights, and even when we fulfil his law this remains so, because all that we do in order to fulfil our part in his covenant is already a gift from him. Only he can purely and simply give, and this he also does.

In this way we have developed to some extent the definition of the supernatural as 'that which surpasses the powers and demands of the creature' by showing how human covenant and human love only

incompletely and imperfectly transcend the powers
and demands of the receiving person, whereas God's
covenant does so completely and perfectly. And yet,
however comprehensively we may have considered
the human starting point of the comparison, we
have not yet established in sufficient detail the degree to which God transcends it. With regard to this
we have three further remarks to make. The first is
that we have in fact been making a comparison between God and the human being *on earth*. It is only
by discussing eternal life that we will be able to
decide whether complete revelation and giving is
there realised, and that among human being mutually, with the body. Let us suppose that this is in
fact the case—a supposition that is justified if only
by realising that the risen body is no longer an
object, but completely taken up into intersubjectivity—then God's revelation and giving still stands
above them, primarily because his revelation and
giving never have to struggle free from a phase of
imperfection. And if the Old Covenant provides man
with an occasion to 'boast of the flesh', of his own
powers and rights, this is the fault of man (which is
why this fundamental temptation always remains)
and to some extent that of the as yet veiled character
of the old dispensation; 'but when a man turns to
the Lord the veil is removed' (2 Cor 3: 16).

But we may also make a second remark which
shows how the covenant between God and man surpasses human interpersonality in an even more
radical way. The human person's self-revelation and
giving always transcend, though in this life never
completely, the obligations and also the forces which
others can apply *to him*; but—and we have already
noted this in passing—not the powers of inner action
by which the personal communication of the other
is received and accepted. For we are able intention-

ally to meet the other person with attention, esteem and gratitude and to experience his or her presence as far as possible. In other words, given that revelation and giving which cannot be compelled from the other, the response of human faith, hope and love lies within our own power. Now it is just in this that we see the difference from our reply in the covenant with God. There even the reply itself surpasses our capacities. We ourselves have to receive the power to accept and take up God's revelation and gift. The very capacities for encounter in faith, hope and love must be given to us, and we call them the infused theological virtues of faith, hope and love. The whole of this life-in-covenant with God, this co-existence with him, must be a participation in God's own life and this is 'the eternal life' or simply 'life', spoken of in the joannine writings, or, as we say today, the life of sanctifying grace. This life, with its capacities for action, does not take the place of those capacities which together with the creature's nature are presupposed by the covenant; on the contrary, these natural capacities are always taken up into the life of grace, their activity is integrated within it and this is 'co-operation' with grace. But the life of grace itself transcends our natural capacities; these are 'raised' to it by an 'infused' life with 'infused' capacities, as theology puts it. In our view this remark contains the most important completion required by the comparisons made previously. Because in his relation to others the human being has the power to accept the other's personal revelation, although he cannot, or can only partially obtain or compel it, we may more correctly say that human personal self-communication lies *outside* the powers and rights of its receiver. That of God, however, lies essentially *above* them, precisely because the capabilities of reception itself must be given together with the gift.

Another person's revelation and gift go beyond my powers and rights, but remain within the equality of one and the same human nature. The revelation and giving of God is not only inter-personal, but also super-natural.

With this second and most important remark concerning the degree to which God's covenant transcends that between human beings there is connected a third remark. This transcendence is continually realised during the whole course of the history of salvation and throughout each person's life of grace. We have just clarified the transcendence of God's covenant by using the idea of 'supernatural'; now, however, we must hasten to return to the idea of 'covenant' precisely in order to illuminate the ever surpassing and thus discontinuous and surprising aspect of God's activity of dialogue. There exists a supernatural covenant with God, but to this we should like to add that there exists no 'supernature'. By this we mean: God's supernatural activity does not result in a whole which as a superstructure—or better, like an upper floor—has a certain independence and regularity of its own, a higher parallel to created nature which, once given, goes on to act further by its own powers and rights. This going *further* on its own powers can partially be the case with covenant between human beings. There one can still grow in a certain measure through one's own reflections on what has been given, but on the other hand the community also demands the communication of that which has not yet been received, or even suspected; surprise, thus, and a bond between persons often dies away through lack of surprises. With God, however, we stand before the ever new surprise, which nevertheless constitutes a continual scandal to the human being's maintenance of his own power, idea and right, as we have already shown above. This discontinuity is apparent in the history of God's covenants which, let us repeat, constitute one covenant, thus in the surprise which the new covenant brings in comparison with the old, but also in that of the progressive sacral phases within the Old Testament itself, and lastly and above all through the completely incalculable and inconceivable breakthrough of God's kingdom in the return of the Lord. Furthermore, in the personal life of every human being there can but be the progress of a continually reviewed and thus surprising divine initiative, and not only through a growth from within in a life of grace given once and for all. One could rightly say that this would be in conflict with the doctrine of merit, namely that of the meriting of an increase of sanctifying grace. That the offer of a new initiative, of a new and deeper love, or in technical terms, of a new actual grace, should be earned has, however, never been defined by the church. One can very well deny it. It is even generally accepted that for an authentically higher level of spiritual life, and consequently for a 'second conversion' which sets that higher spiritual life in motion, an unmerited grace is needed. And it is a point of faith that such a grace is not earned, but only received for that most profound conversion and most sublime development in love which is needed for a christian death, or in other words, for perseverance to the end (Dz 806). So the wholly supernatural character of the covenant never fails to bring with it the most complete form of giving, whence the most complete astonishment by the living God, which is manifested so well in outline by the history of the testaments and in personal life by the adventures of saints and mystics. With this third remark we have completed our description of the measure in which God's covenant surpasses the mutual alliances among human beings. Thereby we have also said enough about God's covenant activity in itself, in contrast to his creation. In our last point in this section, however, we must now demonstrate the unity of both forms of divine activity, in conjunction with what we said in the first point about the unity of making and covenant activity in man.

God's covenant-activity and his creation

That unity we described as a mutual inclusion within themselves of the making of something and the binding of oneself to someone. One always approaches someone through the making of something and conversely the making of something is always ultimately an approach to someone. We can now ascertain the same relation between God's creation and covenant-activity, though it is also on a higher level, which makes the relations between the two essentially different from the corresponding relations on our human, earthly level.

In the first place God's covenant activity includes his creation, and that in two ways which both have something exclusively divine about them. The covenant includes the creation as a presupposition: for there must exist created persons if God wishes to approach them with his covenant. Now this may also be said of every interpersonal activity between human beings, but comparison with that already shows clearly that for God the relations are completely different. For us the other person exists independently of us, we presuppose his existence as an exterior datum; but in God's covenant-activity the person he addresses is presupposed as creature of that same God, which is also why in the covenant God has the sovereign freedom that we have just described. In addition, for us human beings the other person is a pre-supposition, a pre-established datum which also temporally precedes the forming of a human alliance. For God this needs in no way to be the case and the supposition lies solely in the order of necessity, not in that of time.

Yet God's covenant-activity includes his creation not only as a presupposition, but also in a much broader manner. It is itself always creating at the same time, just as we human beings, when we enter into personal alliance with others, also always bring forth something, even if it is only the air-vibrations of a word. So also God creates gifts in us at the same time. He gives himself as uncreated gift, but his unity with us, his presence before us and within us is at the same time a fulfilment of ourselves, a new life with new capacities, as we have briefly described above. Nevertheless, even here there appears a difference from human interpersonality. There the gift is also always a medium and even what is effected in or to the other person's body in relation is sign and also concealment, and can also set itself up as independent. God's gifts of grace, however, are no medium but identical with the bond and presence of himself as reality in us. In themselves the created gifts of grace are purely an *être d'union*, a unity of existence, a co-existence; and the life of grace is purely a life-together-with. Expressing this in terms of action, one can say that therefore the grace to believe, hope and love not only constitutes in us a new capability for action, but at the same time an inward proclamation of the covenant, an inward witness, an inward promise, an inward embrace. St John speaks the same language when he says: 'You have been anointed by the Holy One, and you all know' (1 Jn 2 : 20). Certainly it must be noted here that this life on earth also brings with it the sign in its objective aspect, but this occurs in this way, that God perhaps works in preaching, sacrament, government, etc., through his glorified Christ, but also and as such in Christ's church still living here on earth. Having said this, we have now given sufficient indication of the double way in which God's covenant activity includes his creation, namely as its presupposition and as identical with itself.

Conversely, God's creation also includes his covenant activity; the activity of the covenant is contained within the work of creation. This is evident from what we have just said above. For all covenant activity *is* at the same time creation, and thus materially it falls among God's works of creation, just as all interpersonal activity among human beings can be counted as human making, and—to continue the comparison—just as man himself may be classed among the animal species. This latter point of comparison demonstrates still more clearly than the former that in none of these cases is the most essential aspect brought forth as common denominator. God's covenant activity says much more than his creation; for this reason it also remains at the same time a raising of the creature above his own created nature.

We may thus now proceed to consider creation on its own, disregarding the activity of the covenant (which is at the same time creative), and so compare the two in their distinction from each other. When we thus consider God's actual creation in itself, even then we shall see that it points to his covenant activity, indeed, we believe that one may even say that it supposes God's covenant activity; so that between the two forms of divine activity there is mutual supposition; not only does the covenant suppose the creation (as we have already worked out), but the creation also supposes the covenant. Before justifying our use here of the word 'suppose', however, let us more closely inspect the connection that God's creation has with his covenant. That connection is one of destination. God creates *for* the covenant, *in order* to raise humans further; he creates persons to enter into covenant with him, to make them his children. In the first section of the preceding chapter we have already cited the First Vatican Council's affirmation concerning the aim of God's creation. God creates 'to his glory' (Dz 1805) or 'to show his perfection by the good that he imparts (*impertitur*) to his creatures' (Dz 1783). In our opinion this description of the goal of creation leaves room for the inclusion within it of the raising of the creature, for God manifests his majesty and perfection in the most sublime way precisely in that he imparts to his creatures the highest good he can give them. But even if the Vatican Council's statement were applicable only to the aim of creation in so far as it is implicit in the activity of creating and not related to the raising of the creature, it would in no sense rule out the openness of the whole of creation towards the goal constituted by that exaltation. This will now become more clear as we consider in more detail this orientation of God's creation towards a goal. In doing this we shall first recall what we have said concerning the connection between the making of something and interpersonal activity among human beings. When we compare with this the connection between God's creation and his covenant activity we find that the human relations are surpassed in two aspects; namely by God's freedom and by the manner in which orientation towards the covenant appears in his creation.

Firstly, then, God's freedom. We human beings are also free to direct our making of something towards someone, but this freedom is quite relative. According to our own choice we are able to direct our work towards certain persons, we can serve them or harm them by it, we can make our artefacts the expression of love or hate for this or that person. But there is one thing which we cannot do. We cannot eliminate from our work all relation to persons, to any and every human person. The man who attempts to will not persist in it; but even while he does manage to do so he will not only be serving himself and speaking for and to himself, he will also be taking up a position of aversion towards others. Solitude is not existence without others, but the absence and lack of others with whom one is nevertheless bound up because for us the others are a datum which we cannot eliminate, any more than we can bring it about. Therefore in our production we are (more or less) free to address ourselves to particular people, but we are not free to direct ourselves or not to direct ourselves towards created persons, by virtue of the fact that we are created together with others and others are created with us. That is why in the first point in this section we said that the making of something is always at the same time an orientation towards someone. It is this from greater or less distance, more or less explicitly, but it is this necessarily.

Such is the case with us human beings; such is not the case with God. For he is free in relation to his creature. Not only was he free to create, but once he has created God also retains the same freedom with regard to the creature he has brought into existence. We have given this adequate treatment in the second point of this section. Here it need only be expressed in a fashion in which we spontaneously think of it and which also persists in traditional ecclesiastical terminology. It is this; God could also have created without entering into covenant, without further raising his creature. In our preceding chapter we said that God could have not created. He could exist without his creatures. Now to this we would add, God could also have not raised his creature further; he could have purely and solely created. Man cannot purely and solely make something without directing himself towards someone. God, however, can indeed purely create. Here we have the most pointed human expression of God's freedom.

Nevertheless, this first difference between God's activity and that of human beings must be completed by a second, which points in precisely the opposite direction. God's covenant activity is not only distinguished in the most sublime way from his creation through the fact that the latter could as such also occur alone, but it *also permeates the whole of his creation as its goal*. This relation is primarily evident from the fact, more or less generally accepted by theologians, that even from the very beginning God has exalted man. Let us temporarily disregard this simultaneity, however, for the connection is deeper still. Even if human existence had been raised 'later', it would still remain true that orientation towards this exaltation was engraved in the creation from the beginning as its sense and goal. We are speaking now of the creation as it is in fact, not of that possible, but non-existent 'pure' creation to which we referred above. It is true of this factual creation, however, that orientation towards exaltation is inwardly contained by it.

Here also we perceive a difference from our human activity. We human beings are able to give a purpose to something or even in a certain measure to someone; we can use a flower vase as a rubbish-bin and we can give another person a task. This does not necessarily involve the use of force or violence, but it certainly takes place *a posteriori*, i.e., the existence of that something or that someone is given,

146

and hence the bestowing of purpose is always extrinsic to its essence. In making things, however, we can always destine them for something: a vase for flowers and a clock to show the time. But even here the purpose we bestow is not completely intrinsic. Just as our artefacts suppose the materials, so also they suppose the utility immanent in those materials; and just as our human fabrication is a changing and even a combining, so the purposiveness of our product is constructed from the already present immanent finality of our materials.

God, however, makes out of nothing, without pre-existing material, and thus also without the datum of an already existent and thus independent purpose in something or someone. Creation proceeds entirely from him: his intention is also expressed without hindrance. He makes the creature in the whole of its reality, and thus in the whole of its purposiveness and utility. Orientation towards the covenant and exaltation is therefore intrinsic to the creature. If we return for a moment to the possible but non-existent pure creation we see that it differs from the factual creation precisely in its lack of internal orientation towards the raising of the creature's existence. So, furthermore, we cannot say of this possible creation that it supposes the covenant. Of the actual creation, however, we can certainly say this, and we believe that the intrinsic orientation has now also justified the proposition we put forward above, namely that creation supposes the covenant. Of course, it has also become clear that here we do not mean the same as was intended when we said that the covenant supposes the creation. The covenant supposes the creation as foundation, as basis, as point of departure (these terms must be interpreted neither temporally nor spatially), but creation supposes the covenant as purpose. One might be tempted to remark here that in the latter case the word 'suppose' is not being used in its real meaning, that it does not mean the same as 'presuppose'. Yet to us this certainly appears to be the case, precisely because purposiveness is intrinsic to the creature. For this reason the creature's purpose is just as basic as its existence, and the (actually existing) creature subsists, partly through its orientation towards the goal, whose achievement is nevertheless completely free.

All of this may be developed in more detail if we compare the created realities of nature and grace with each other. In conclusion let us now return once more to God's own activities. We find ourselves looking for a term to express the orientation, contained within God's creation, towards the covenant. We might say that he is already calling as he creates and that every created person is at the same time called into the community of the covenant with him. Perhaps it is better, however, to reserve the verb 'to call' for an activity that is already interpersonal, thus by which the personal nature of the creature is presupposed and not constituted; in doing so we should be following what scripture seems to do. And then for creation we should have rather to seek a term indicating unilateral activity, but one which also includes purposiveness. It seems to us that we find this in the verb 'to destine'. As he creates, God already destines us for his covenant, he destines us to be called, creates us such that that call is a completely unmerited gift and in order to truly perceive it we must still receive from him a capacity to hear.

In this case, however, the motive which will presently lead to the covenant is already active in the creation itself, and that motive is love. God creates out of love. In our previous chapter we did not express this because scripture does not say it, nor do the pronouncements of the teaching authority of the church connect the creation with God's love, at the most only with his *bontias* and *liberalitas*, his goodness and generosity. Yet it is not unusual for the christian to ascribe the creation to God's love. We believe that there is a reason for this, as also for the reserve of scripture and teaching authority. Naturally, in basing itself more or less consciously upon biblical terminology, the teaching authority will not have explicitly connected God's love with his creation. And scripture itself seems to conceive of 'love' as interpersonal, as a community supposing persons. as is expressed by the famous remark of St Gregory the Great: 'minus quam inter duo caritas esse non potest'. If we now wish on the one hand to speak about a creation out of love and on the other to maintain the original, interpersonal meaning of this word, then it seems to us that precisely as participants in the covenant we may say: God created (in fact, that is, not in unrealised possibility) out of love, because he created for the covenant. The bible appears to express this view once, but on the basis of God's *hesed*, his grace, which is after all primarily a gift of the covenant. This occurs in Psalm 136 (135), in which the refrain in each verse, 'for his steadfast love endures for ever' is related mainly to his activities of covenant and salvation, but also to God's creation (vv. 5–9). Here we shall conclude what we hope has been a sufficiently detailed discussion of God's creation and covenant.

4
Jesus' signs

It is noteworthy that Jesus only once refused a miracle. On innumerable occasions, however, as the gospels show us, he performed them. Requested or unrequested, he gives his signs, and on several occasions he explicitly calls on them as evidence. Thus he raises the paralytic 'that you may know that the Son of man has authority on earth to forgive sins' (Mk 2 : 10 = Mt 9 : 6 = Lk 5 : 24). He says, 'But if it is by the Spirit of God that I cast out demons, then the kingdom of God has come upon you' (Mt 12 : 28 = Lk 11 : 20). He heals the man born blind 'that the works of God might be made manifest in him' (Jn 9 : 3), and asks his Father to let him raise Lazarus from death 'that they may believe that thou didst send me' (Jn 11 : 42). Consequently 'he began to upbraid the cities where most of his mighty works had been done, because they did not repent' (Mt 11 : 20) and, looking back over the whole of his preaching, he says at the Last Supper, 'If I had not done among them the works which no one else did, they would not have sin; but now they have seen and hated both me and my Father' (Jn 15 : 24). Therefore, in his sermon at Pentecost, Peter calls Jesus 'a man attested to you by God with mighty works and wonders and signs which God did through him in your midst' (Acts 2: 22; cf 10: 38). John, who expressly connects sign and faith on numerous occasions in his gospel, says at the end of it: 'these (signs) are written that you may believe that Jesus is the Christ, the Son of God, and that believing you may have life in his name' (Jn 20: 31). The conclusion of Mark also relates the signs wrought by the apostles to the glorified Lord, who thereby himself 'confirmed the message' (Mk 16: 20). Hence it is that these apostles, like their master, sometimes make appeal to the signs (2 Cor 12; Rm 15: 18f.; Heb 2: 3f.).

The texts cited here refer more or less exclusively to miracles in the strict sense, i.e., to signs which are achieved through an intervention in the physical world. However, Jesus does not restrict himself to the bringing about of such signs, but is himself set as a sign (Lk 2: 34). So by 'signs' we understand more than just miracles. Let us give a general description of the sign by proceeding from a distinction which is fundamental in this book. We have distinguished between that which others can by their own power ascertain in a person and that which can only be known by being freely communicated by the person himself and freely accepted in trust by the others, thus between the sphere of evidence and ascertainment and the sphere of revelation and faith; in other words, the sphere of objectivity and that of intersubjectivity or interpersonality. For Israel and for Christ—and for every man in so far as he lives in Christ—this latter sphere at the same time contains the secret of a supernatural relationship with God. In a first approach we should now like to describe the sign as something that leads our cognition from the first sphere to the second. In saying this we have already given the idea of sign more specificity than

it has according to the customary scholastic definition 'something which brings knowledge of something else' as explained by the well-known example
of smoke as a sign of the presence of fire. In the sense
which we are here attaching to it, the sign leads not
to the knowledge of something, but of someone else,
and precisely in so far as the other is no longer an
ascertainable something, but a self-communicating
someone. A possible example of this is the look or
gift that is the sign of love. It seems to us a good idea
to elaborate the nature of this sign whilst still in the
realm of philosophy, in the same way as we have
already several times indicated the categories proper
to the interpersonal sphere. One might opt in favour
of using a separate word for the interpersonal sign,
for example, 'symbol'. We shall not do so here because we doubt whether this is in agreement with
general usage, and especially because the theological
idea which we wish to introduce by means of this
reflection is expressed by the scriptural word 'sign'.
We may now proceed at once to this theological idea
by expressly naming the supernatural bond with
God. The sign of which we are speaking is therefore
something ascertainable which leads us to the knowledge of someone's attachment to God, and in particular to their mission from God. In the case of
Jesus the sign is so ascertainable that it makes him
known as the Christ and the Son of God.

Nevertheless, this theological definition is still too
broad for our present purpose. It applies to all that
Jesus says in self-revelation and to the whole activity by which he introduces and emphasises what
he says. But even in our philosophical description we
were too general. Here we do not need to consider
all interpersonal signs, but only one category. We
are able to communicate a truth directly, principally
in words, and in addition bear it out with other

signs. So there are signs which are direct expressions and signs which are at their service, in that they demonstrate the truth of their expression. Scholasticism talks about formal and instrumental signs; here, let us say, expressive and demonstrative signs. It is clear that this distinction only has sense with respect to those signs which proceed from a human being: the fire announces and at the same time proves its existence by the smoke. Now it might be thought that within human interaction this distinction only finds a meaning when related to communication concerning matters outside the partners in the dialogue: thus a person may communicate a scientific discovery and accompany it with various forms of proof of his competence and honesty. But also in the case of a strictly personal communication to a community demonstrative signs can, and even must, be given. Even when a person signifies his love to someone, he will also have to demonstrate his reliability. All communication of the person by means of the body is, at least in this world, always incomplete and at the same time conceals, even to such a degree that it is the masters of expression, artists, who have the most acute experience of the way in which all their signs fall short. Moreover, man can also deliberately use the distance between sign and content in order to hide, and abuse it in order to lie and deceive. Even self-communication knows forms of false appearance; faith in someone's love for me is not only the most sublime but also the most hazardous form of human faith. Here is certainly where demonstrative sign will be most intimately conjoined with expressive sign, where both will be woven together into a single message which is in fact a coexistence; but the possibility of deception nevertheless reveals that a real distinction can occur between them. We must therefore have the sense and humility both to expect and to provide these signs in our relations with others.

Now Jesus participated in human interrelation, and in his message we may therefore distinguish expressive signs and demonstrative signs. We are induced to do so by the remarks we quoted above from him and his apostles. Certainly God spoke in him, God who, as Vatican I says in its *Dogmatic Constitution on Catholic Faith*, 'can neither be deceived nor even himself deceive' (Dz 1789). However, that council immediately adds:

> In order that the obedience of our faith should nevertheless be in agreement with reason, God desired to join to the inward graces of the Holy Spirit external proofs of his revelation, namely divine acts, and in the first place wonders and prophecies, which by abundantly demonstrating God's omnipotence and omniscience are most sure signs of divine revelation, adapted to the insight of everyone. That is why Moses and the prophets and above all Christ the Lord himself wrought many clear miracles and prophecies [Dz 1790].

Of himself God does not bring any risk into our faith in him, but risks do enter it through the fact that he uses human beings as his mouthpiece, and indeed, even in so far as he makes his eternal Word incarnate. Of course, even in his human nature God's Son can neither deceive nor be deceived. But, in the first place, he speaks with the words of men. Secondly, he adapts himself to us since we can only assimilate his revelation partially and gradually. In the Old Testament God had 'spoken in many and various ways by the prophets' (Heb 1: 1), but even his definitive revelation in the Son comes to us during that Son's earthly life in a corresponding manner. Finally, he 'on whose lips no guile was found' (1 Pet 2 : 22) was even willing to adapt himself to the untruthfulness of our society and to distinguish himself by signs from the 'false Christs and false prophets' against whom he warns (Mk 13 : 22 = Mt 24 : 24). This willingness of God's Son to give demonstrative signs belongs to the concrete way in which he became and remained man during his life on earth, divested, namely, of his external equality with God, in the form of a servant. We may most certainly feel astonished at this; in fact the believer would be wronging his faith in some way if his astonishment were not constantly aroused by this divine condescension. We may not believe that what God himself has accepted is unworthy of him. If the use of demonstrative signs between human beings is an act of common sense and humility, the acceptance of these signs in Christ finds its grounds in the belief that as man 'he humbled himself' (Phil 2 : 8).

Refusing the signs on grounds of an appeal to God is one extreme, but another is to demand it on the basis of an appeal to humanity. At first one might say that the necessity of demonstrative signs in human relations justifies such a demand, even of Christ. Nevertheless, the fact that he sometimes refuses miracles must make us careful of this contention. We must first and foremost be concerned with the miracle as a sign, not as the means of generally satisfying any other need. Thus Jesus accuses the crowd at Capernaum, 'you seek me, not because you saw signs, but because you ate your fill of the loaves' (Jn 6 : 26), and to Herod who, undoubtedly out of lust for sensation, 'was hoping to see some miracle done by him' (Lk 23 : 8) he said not a word. But even when man is concerned with the miracle as a sign he may in no sense set requirements as regards its nature and number of occurrences. 'An evil and adulterous generation seeks for a sign; but no sign shall be given to it except the sign of the prophet Jonah' (Mt 12: 39; Lk 11: 29). Mark (8: 11f) narrates that this answer was preceded by the specific demands for a sign from heaven—as we should say today, a miracle that once and for all excludes all doubt—and in his version Jesus' reply sounds even more decisive, 'No sign shall be given to this generation.' The signs already given are sufficient for those who have understanding and good will, hence elsewhere Jesus accuses, 'You know how to interpret the appearance of the sky, but you cannot interpret the signs of the times' (Mt 16: 3), after which the statement about the sign of Jonah is repeated. The whole presence of the Lord previously had thus already been a sign, and it must suffice. Indeed, for a developed faith just the personality of Jesus can suffice, without physical wonders, as is supposed in his saying, 'even if you do not believe me, believe the works' (Jn 10: 38; cf also 14: 11). From all this it is clear that there may be no question of demanding a sign. It is very much more the case that in his whole attitude man must continually recognise that every demonstrative sign of God's revelation shares in the unearned nature of that revelation, that it is a gift in the same way as is revelation. By virtue of the relations in man and between men, which were described above, one may justifiably *ask* for signs, but this must remain a request which leaves the nature and number to God, to Christ. A sign is not a condition which is demanded because the reason will not otherwise surrender, but a help which is asked that a person *may* believe.

In saying this we are already saying that a sign is addressed not only to the understanding but at the same time to the will, that it must be received by a freely accepting mind. One must be open to it; one can close oneself to it. We have called the sign something which leads from the sphere of evidence and ascertainment to that of revelation and faith. But it does not do this automatically. The sphere of free acceptance cannot be entered other than by freely accepting, one cannot arrive at faith except by actually believing. It is true that the demonstrative sign, like the expressive sign, is ascertainable, and indeed, that purely in its sensory perceptibility it forces itself upon a person. If one is present, one cannot overlook the fact (it will nevertheless be remembered that with facts which reach us via an historical witness the relation is more complex). But in order further to recognise this fact as a sign, the freedom of faith is needed. Faced by a purely expressive sign one can, given certain conditions—for instance, that one understands the language—discern its content, but even then it is possible to say with Faust: 'Die Botschaft hör' ich wohl, allein mir fehlt der Glaube' (Full well I hear the message, it is but faith I lack). But neither is this faith compelled by the demonstrative sign. This sign brings us nearer to believing, it presents a more insistent invitation to do so; but it always remains the vehicle of an invitation, it never becomes the instrument of compulsion. Here we again see the essence of the interhuman sign. Even a sign which proceeds from a thing has often to be interpreted by a certain particular form of cognition, namely by induction, which is always based upon a certain disposition, a connaturality, a congeniality. But with the sign that a person voluntarily gives there is always the necessity that it be interpreted in freedom.

To this philosophical view of the recognition of signs we must add a few further points in order to avoid misunderstanding. It might be objected that we are trapped in a vicious circle: a person believes by virtue of the demonstrative signs, but these signs must themselves be believed in turn. But this circle is not vicious, it is rather unavoidable and normal. We might compare it to the following: we understand something because we understand that we must understand it. To put this in a negative way: our insight never depends on something that goes beyond our insight, our knowledge never depends on something outside our knowledge (in the measure that will or feeling are in action here, they determine our knowledge by the awareness we have of their movement). Yet the reasoning may hardly be called circular, since it now appears that in its purest moment our knowledge knows its content and *at the same time* illuminates itself. And what has been said here of our knowledge as a whole also holds in some measure for certain of its spheres. We may say that our sensory knowledge cannot be grounded without reference to our senses, and we have already proposed that our believing is not justified outside of our faith. But the statement is only partially true of these limited spheres of knowledge. Our sensory knowledge and also the knowledge of our faith, for example, can be controlled in a negative manner by our logical insight: that which is truly a contradiction cannot be perceived and may not be believed. A control is always present, especially with our free knowledge, our belief. The freedom in which it is achieved brings responsibility. Those who do not accept Jesus' miracles are guilty (Mt 11:20–24=Lk 10:12–15; Jn 15:24), like those who hinder the natural knowledge of God within themselves (Rm 1:20), and we may add like the person who does not believe an honest man. But this implies that in every decision of faith one sees that one can and may and must believe, and thus that one does well in believing and evil in not believing. An element of insight into the truth of what one is about to believe is therefore always present, and in fact precedes the actual believing. So that in the case of disbelief, as Paul so splendidly puts it, 'the truth is suppressed' or 'stifled' (. . . qui veritatem in iniustitia detinent . . . *tōn tēn alētheian en adikia katechontōn*, Rm 1:18). On the other hand, however, it is therefore not the content of a complete knowledge that is thus 'suppressed' or 'stifled', but the first announcement of such a content, as insight which will most fully become our insight only in the act of believing. By adding these remarks about faith itself, we hope to have added support for our philosophical view of faith in signs. Even the signs which demonstrate that one can, may and must believe, must themselves be believed.

It is not without reason that we have emphasised our development so far of a philosophical viewpoint. For, theologically speaking, we are not yet finished. Applied to the signs of the prophets, of the apostles, and of Christ, this view that they must be accepted at least with human faith, that the natural, human reason is not forced into seeing that here divine revelation is present and divine faith must be given. Now, however, a second question poses itself. Do Christ's signs suppose not only human but also divine faith? Can they be accepted in an act (of faith) of the natural reason alone or must one also be enabled by grace to arrive at divine faith in order to be capable of understanding them? It is beyond all doubt that Christ's signs are addressed to human reason and can be recognised by it. For, as is apparent when all things are considered, and as Vatican I expressly states, they are given 'in order that the obedience of our faith should be in agreement with reason' (Dz 1790). The apologists of all times have, with respect to reason, appealed to these signs in order to demonstrate how reasonable it is to accept Christ and his revelation. During the nineteenth century the church gave this appeal to reason protection against those who—tired by the struggle with rationalism—considered this argument from reason as inadmissible and expected help from grace alone; such as Bautain (Dz 1626). But even in a rejection of rationalism, occurring in Pius ix's encyclical *Qui pluribus* of 9th November 1846, human reason is explicitly attributed the task of investigating the fact of God's revelation and its capacity to see with certainty that God is speaking is also acknowledged (Dz 1637–39). Is there talk in these documents of the reason *alone*, apart—at least in principle—from any supernatural aid? They certainly speak of reason in as much as it precedes the act of believing (Dz 1626, 1639), but the question as to whether the grace of faith can be absent here remains unanswered. The expression 'the reason alone' does not appear in Roman documents[1] until halfway through the present century, in the encyclical *Humani generis* of 12th August 1950. This says—in a subordinate clause, moreover—that the divine origin of christianity can be demonstrated from the signs 'by the natural light of reason alone' (Dz 2305). Here we may see—taking into account the authority carried by this document, moreover—an affirmative answer to our question.[2] Yes, man can understand Christ's signs solely with the aid of natural reason.

[1] At one point it is even conspicuously absent: compare point 4 of the Roman decree quoted in Dz 1627 with the previous points.

[2] The text of *Humani generis* reads as follows: 'Quin immo mens humana difficultates interdum pati potest etiam in certo iudicio "credibilitatis" efformando circa catholicam fidem, quamvis tam multa ac mira signa externa divinitus disposita sint quibus vel solo naturali rationis lumine divina christianae religionis origo certo probari possit'. In my opinion one would be overestimating

this passage were one to try to read in it a formal condemnation of the opinion of some theologians, namely that for the recognition of the credibility of divine revelation from the signs a *grace* of faith is justly and theoretically necessary. Since (1) In this encyclical we have rather a warning against a mentality that a condemnation of clearly defined opinions; a series of opinions is referred to rather than precisely formulated (Dz 2318f.) and these are qualified as 'errors or dangerously near error' (*errores vel erroris pericula*); (2) The view against which the cited text directs itself is not among these rejected opinions; (3) The contention of the necessity in principle of the grace of faith is rejected in a subordinate statement, in passing, whilst the main sentence and its context is intended to bring out something else, namely the moral and factual necessity of grace and revelation for insights which in principle can be attained by the reason alone; (4) In an address at the occasion of the 25th anniversary of the College of the Discalced Carmelites in Rome on 23rd September 1951, Pope Pius XII said the following about the encyclical *Humani generis*: 'We have heard, not without painful astonishment, that some have taken this document somewhat amiss, as if we had thereby wished to suppress the research required by the progress of the sciences and to forbid the separate opinions concerning which exchange of thought without danger to faith has up until now been possible in the philosophical and theological schools. Such people have been deceived or have deceived themselves. It was not our intention to lay bonds upon that which is free' (AAS 43 (1951)). Now the opinion that a grace of faith is necessary for the forming of a judgement of credibility on the basis of the signs was counted among the free opinions before *Humani generis*. For all these reasons it appears to us that there can be no question of a formal condemnation of this proposition. Nevertheless, the subordinate clause quoted gives an indication to the contrary. The theologian will therefore have to ask himself whether he can attribute to 'the natural light of reason alone' a recognition of the signs, a formation of the judgement of credibility. It seems to us that this is difficult for those who consider human nature to be exactly the same in this factual order as in a possible *status naturae purae*, even when in both cases they attribute to it a natural desire of a supernatural goal, a desire which only sees that goal as a pure possibility, however, and which therefore only extends under a condition ('if God wills') to the raising up to that goal. We, on the contrary, have already maintained that in this factual order nature is destined by God for an ultimate supernatural goal and is inwardly orientated towards it, that it therefore differs from a possible

This accessibility to reason of Jesus' signs may be termed a limit-case on two grounds. First because our reason is often hindered in its correct function by man's sinful tendency to 'suppress the truth'. Morally, therefore, he needs grace so that, freed from sinful prejudices, he may recognise God's revelation in Christ through the signs. This is shown fully by the context from which we borrowed the words of *Humani generis*.

But there is a second reason for calling this accessibility to reason alone a limit-case. For the sign also retains a function with regard to the person who has already accepted faith. Christ gives signs not only before but also in faith, not only in order to bring the unbeliever to faith but also to lead the believer further to more profound encounter. This is worth illustrating with a few examples from the gospels. When a paralytic is laid down before Jesus (Mk 2 : 1–12 = Mt 9 : 1–8 = Lk 5 : 17–26), he answers the faith of the bearers and of the paralytic himself not with a miracle but with the forgiving of sins, but before the disbelief of the scribes he expressly sets the healing as a sign of the authenticity of that forgiveness. In particular, John mentions several times

---

natura pura by this inner orientation. The latter becomes aware of itself as a natural desire not for a possible supernatural goal, but for that which God has in fact posited and realised in Christ; not conditioned but an absolute desire, for God wishes to exalt us; nevertheless, an absolute desire for this exaltation as gift, as grace and therefore in no way a requirement. This desire can be known by nature as it is, however, and solely with the light of its reason, because it is immanent within this nature itself. Now it also appears to us that with its reason alone human nature can observe the fulfilment of this concretely orientated desire as manifested in signs, and thus that it can discern the factual existence of God's revelation and its credibility from the signs. This nevertheless only concerns a judgement regarding revelation as a whole, not its exact content.

not only that faith is the fruit of Jesus' signs (Jn 2: 11; 3: 2; 4: 53; 7: 31; 9: 30–38; 11: 45; 20: 31), but also that faced with unbelievers the Lord appeals to his signs. Over and against this there remains the fact that Jesus on several occasions supposes, even requires faith before a miracle, a fact to which the apologetical function of the sign must not make us blind. The cases in which we have seen Jesus refuse a miracle show how he sometimes does not wish to set a sign before unbelief. Matthew (13: 58) tells us that in Nazareth Jesus 'did not do many mighty works, on account of their unbelief', and Mark (6: 5) even says that he *could* not do many miracles there. Also he sometimes reproves the unbelief of those who ask for a cure, such as the official at Capernaum (Jn 4: 48) or the father of the epileptic youth (Mk 9: 19–23 =Mt 17: 17=Lk 9: 41); or also the small measure of his own disciples' faith (Mk 4: 40=Mt 8: 26=Lk 8: 25; Mt 14: 31; 17: 20). All of this might apply to the element of unwillingness that inheres in unbelief. It becomes clear that through his signs Jesus is addressing faith, however, when he praises and blesses it, before his miracles, as in the case of the centurion (Mt 8: 10=Lk 7: 9), or after them, in saying 'your faith has made you well' to the man cured of his blindness, Bartimaeus (Mk 10: 52 = Mt 9: 29), to the leper (Lk 17: 19) or to the woman who had touched his garment (Mk 5: 34=Mt 9: 22=Lk 8: 48). This last fact is narrated to us by the synoptics as an interruption in the story of the raising of Jairus' daughter. Now the bringing together of these two miracles into one story can teach us a lot. Firstly the contrast between Jesus' mode of action in the two miracles: he himself allows that of the woman with the haemorrhage to be in public, but is willing to raise the dead girl in the presence only of her parents and of the three disciples who were with him on

Mount Tabor and in the Garden of Olives. This tells us that a miracle is sometimes intended only for certain believers and designed to bring them a specific message. Furthermore, it is remarkable that the synoptic evangelists, who are so fond of listing events after one another as in a catalogue, have here respected the weaving together of the two events in their story. The fathers of the church saw a symbol of the history of salvation in this story of the two miracles: in history Christ is on his way to Israel, but first he heals the heathens of their impurity before going on to awaken his own people from the sleep of death. It is not improbable that this exegesis develops what the gospels themselves are intended to suggest here. With this we may complete what we said a little earlier. For the person who already believes the demonstrative sign can become an expressive sign. We could go into this in more detail, partly in the gospels themselves, but let us content ourselves with a treatment of miraculous signs.

Up to this point we have made a few remarks concerning Christ's signs in general. Although the texts we have cited all speak about miracles, our intention was nevertheless to consider the idea of the sign more broadly. For besides the miracles the prophecies, or rather, their fulfilment, must also be mentioned as demonstrative signs of Jesus' messiahship. And thirdly we have met texts which in some way present the Lord himself as a sign. Here let us treat the first of these three forms of sign: the miracle.

The miracle

A creation of belief by the first christian community can no more be the explanation of the originality of the miracle stories than it can be that of the originality of Jesus' whole personality. In our view we do not need further to support the historicity in detail, seeing that we are not directly engaged in apologetics; for today many are inclined to deny its actual occurrence precisely because they think that there is a contradiction within the very idea of a miracle. It is even more important for dogmatics to become clear as to the essence of the miracle, so as to give it its place among the other signs and in the whole dialogue between God and man in Christ. To avoid becoming one-sided we shall first consult what scripture and tradition have to say on the subject.[1]

Naturally the first thing that strikes us about Christ's miracles is their exceptional character. We have the curing of incurables: lepers, paralytics and the blind; we have the driving out of demons, which perhaps includes a psychic healing; and all these healings take place instantaneously; finally, mention is made of three occasions on which someone is brought back to life: Jairus' daughter (Mk 5: 41f. = Mt 9: 25 = Lk 8: 54f.); the young man from Nain (Lk 7: 14f.) and Lazarus (Jn 11: 43f.). This raising of the dead seldom occurs, while healing, in con-

[1] We owe much of what follows to the apologetics course of our teacher from F. M. Malmberg, sj. The theses of his unpublished treatise are to be found in a psychological–personalist version by J. M. Kijm, sj: 'Apologetische notities bij het wonder', in *Bijdragen der Nederlandse Jezuiten* 14 (1953), 148–155. The blondelian inspiration of these theses may be found in more detail in two publications: Pierre de Locht, 'Maurice Blondel et sa controverse au sujet du miracle', *Ephemerides Theologiae Lovanienses* 30 (1954), 344; 390; and F. Taymans, sj, 'Le miracle, signe du surnaturel', *Nouvelle Revue Théologique* 77 (1955), 225–245. For the relation between the miracle and the laws of nature, see: B. van Leeuwen, ofm, 'Wonder en natuurorde' *Jaarboek 1953 van het Werkgenootschap van kath. theologen in Nederland*, Gooi & Sticht, Hilversum, 1953, 5–13; and for the religious context of the miracle: J. De Fraine, sj 'Het ethos der evangelische wonderverhalen' *Streven 13* (1945), 1–10. For a fuller treatment, see L. Monden, sj, *Het Wonder*, Sheed & Ward, Antwerp 1955.

trast, takes place numerous times; but even this accumulation of healings is a rare event in the history of mankind. Therefore, in the first place, we are astonished by these exceptional facts, and this is also the reaction of the eyewitnesses themselves, as the evangelists often mention: 'And immediately they were overcome with amazement' (Mk 5: 42); 'Fear seized them all' (Lk 7: 16). But these wonders are not only presented to us as startling or astonishing. Sometimes they are expressly referred to by Jesus as a sign of his teaching and activity. Or they give the impression of a charitable deed: 'He has done all things well' (Mk 7: 37); 'He went about doing good' (Acts 10: 38). Not only astonishment, but awe, respect, fear of God, fill the witnesses, together with gratitude and joy. In the gospels the miracle does not appear to us purely as an exceptional fact that might equally be a process of nature, but as a sign of God's special, loving presence in Jesus: 'A great prophet has arisen among us and God has visited his people!' (Lk 7: 16). The impression we are given by these stories is already suggested by the words the evangelists use for Jesus' miracles. The impression of exception and astonishment is contained in the term 'miracles' (usually *terata*; once *thaumasia*, Mt 21: 15; once *paradoxa*, Lk 5: 26; Vulgate *prodigia*, sometimes *portenta* or *mirabilia*; the classical word in the Latin treatises, *miracula*, does not appear in the New Testament Vulgate). A strong suggestion of divine origin lies in the term 'mighty works', *dynameis* (Vulgate *virtutes*; literally: 'powers') and in 'works', *erga* (Vulgate *opera*), the latter term being favoured especially by John. Most characteristic, however, and appearing most often both in the synoptics and in John is the term 'signs', *sēmeia* (Vulgate *signa*). This last term speaks for itself; it may be mentioned here that for John it has the particular meaning of a symbol which proclaims Jesus' majesty: '. . . the first of his signs Jesus did at Cana in Galilee, and manifested his glory' (Jn 2:11).

The elements of the miracle which may be found in the gospels also remain in the tradition of the church; nevertheless, in her preaching, and above all in her theology, a strong shift of emphasis is to be noted. Putting things broadly, the patristic accent is upon the miracle's symbolic function, while from Anselm onwards the scholastic accent is upon its exceptional character. Let us take St Augustine as representing the fathers; his doctrine concerning miracles is to be found mainly in his sermons on the fourth gospel. The first impression one gets is that he is minimising the aspect of exceptionality. According to Augustine God performs deeds within the usual course of nature which are no less mighty than miracles; rather mightier, in fact. Christ changes the water into wine at Cana, but God continually brings it about that rain makes grapes grow on the vine. Christ multiplies the loaves, but God repeatedly causes an ear of corn with many grains on it to grow out of one grain. Christ raises several people to life, but God gives life to so many daily. The daily deeds of power no longer attract our attention, and therefore he does unusual works of wonder (in Johannis evangelium tract. VIII, 1: PL 35, 1450). So for St Augustine the miracle is in the first place a sign which by its striking nature proclaims God's special action, a sign which makes us attentive to his presence. But in addition the miracle is a symbolic token of the whole of Christ's work of salvation. In his comparison of the miracle with the other works of God, Augustine is being original, but this originality makes him all the more forcefully return to that symbolism which is classical of the fathers. The deeds of the incarnate Word are themselves words; we must therefore listen to the language of the miracles. The changing of water into wine signifies the succeeding of the Old Testament by the New. And so they go on, Augustine and all the fathers, with a rich feeling for symbolism that sometimes slips into a subjective allegorism which has given their name somewhat less respect among us—wrongly, moreover, because it is only incidental.

This accent upon the symbolic aspect disappears, however, from St Anselm onwards. At least in reflective theology; preaching will remain patristically inspired for a long while. All attention now turns to the exceptionality. It is no longer the aim of the miracle that stands in the foreground, but its efficient cause, God, God alone. Now no continuity exists between God's customary works and his miracles, but a radical division. According to Anselm there are three efficient causes; nature, free will, and God. Nature and free will do nothing independently of God, but God does work independently of nature and the will of men, and such is the case with the miracle. He explains this in speaking about the virginal conception of Jesus (*Liber de conceptu virginis et de originali peccato,* c. 11; PL 158, col. 445f.) which already implies that such an invisible work of God as this, which is therefore in itself no sign, is reckoned among God's miracles. A similar conception of the miracle is found at the many places where St Thomas speaks of it (cf especially 3 CG, 100–102; STh I, 105, 6–8; 110, 4; 114, 4; I, II, 113; II, II, 178; III, 43f.). Yet, in contrast with Anselm, Thomas does not equate the act of creation with a miracle. He also seems to exclude only that the creature should act by his own power in the case of a miracle, not that God may raise him to be his instrument. However, miracles remain works of God that lie not just outside the order of one single creature, but outside that of the whole of created nature. They are divided according to that exceptionality, and it is through this that we come to see that God is at work and wishes thus to provide a guarantee for a teaching or a person sent by him. The emphasis upon the exceptional nature which God's activity shows has since remained in the theology of the miracle, particularly in apologetic proofs on the basis of miracles. It was only in the last century, with Newman and Blondel, that it was realised that the symbolic function includes more than the exceptional nature of the miracle.

This last sentence shows the exact difference between the theological views on miracles which we have sketched. It is not that scholasticism sees the miracle purely as an exception, and that, in contrast the fathers and some more recent theologians consider it as a sign. In the miracle each sees a sign; which is why we heard miracles included by the First Vatican Council among the signs of revelation. The point at which they diverge is in answering the question 'What makes the miracle a sign?' What we may term the scholastic view would answer, 'Its exceptional character, and that alone.' It is obvious that, in contrast, the fathers did not attribute such a value to this aspect as did scholasticism, and a more recent tendency is attempting to express their view by saying that it is not only its exceptional character that makes the miracle a sign, but also the whole religious context in which it takes place. We should like to make this our own position. It seems to be provisionally justified by the various elements which the evangelical accounts of miracles appeared to contain. Upon closer inspection these will all be seen to be essential elements, since an exceptional character can also be attributed to something which is merely a rarity, a natural event, or also to a sign of the devil or antichrist, a pseudo-miracle. There must therefore also be a religious connection to complete the symbolic character. Now there are nevertheless certain theologians who will resist such an 'underestimation' of the exceptional nature of the miracle. They believe that there do occur clear exceptions to the laws of nature which of themselves already refer unequivocally to God as their cause. It is therefore necessary for us to go somewhat more deeply into the relation between miracle, creation and the laws of nature. After this we shall be free to describe the other element, the religious element which makes the miracle a sign.

From St Augustine we have heard that God's power is no less when he is governing the ordinary course of things than in a miracle. Now in the usual run of events God also uses creatures as causes. If this takes away nothing of his power, then it is not impossible that in his miracles he also uses created causes, even though they may be other than the usual ones, and more concealed. We are even certain that this is the case and see here an application of what we said earlier (p. 100) about the relation between God's activity and that of his creatures. Through his universal causation, we wrote, God causes the creature to act, but then it is also the creature itself that acts:

'Here he is the one who does everything, by giving creatures all their activity, by making it real, by allowing creatures, or better, by causing them, to act in everything. But God also makes the creature itself act; he realises the creature itself as acting under its own power and according to its own laws and as itself causing the result, its activity. Although for the relation between the actions of two creatures, at least in so far as they are physical, it may be true that what the one does the other need not do, and thus also that what one does more the other needs to do less, when it comes to the relation between God and creature there can be no such talk. On the contrary, there it is the case that what God does, the creature also does; what God does not do, neither does the creature; that which God does more, the creature also does more; that which God does less, the creature also does less.'

This development of the faith in creation justifies us in also accepting the presence and activity of created causes in the case of the miracle, even though these may be further concealed from us. We believe that God never 'creates something in addition' in the purely quantitative sense of this expression. Though in God's activity with created causes one can certainly distinguish creation as a particular moment, in so far as God causes what is new in it (cf pp. 97–8), but this is present in all God's actions, not only in the miracle. There it is simply more striking.

What we have deduced from the relation between creator and creature may also be concluded from the incarnation of the Word. Christ's divine working never hinders his human activity in anything, and it may be expected that this relation with his own humanity extends to those around him, even in the case of his miracles. For all these reasons we are not in agreement with Anselm's tripartite division. Material nature and human freedom do not act without God, but the converse of this is just as true. The miracle is not an act of God alone, completely apart from his creation. This frees us from any need to try and establish exactly what the forces of nature are capable of achieving, or at least that which they are not able to achieve. The possibility of 'unknown forces' being active in a miracle must not be denied, but rather affirmed, and the right to seek out these forces even in the miracle must not be denied to the exponent of experimental science. Equally, a miracle is not explained in this way let alone explained away. That for which natural science may seek an explanation is the actual physical occurrence of the miracle, but even when this is found the symbolic function is in no way removed, as we shall argue with more emphasis presently.

There are two ways in which our present contention might be misunderstood. It might now be said that the miracle is also being explained *only* in terms of natural causes, and its exceptional character might be denied. We believe that neither of these two opinions follow from our view. As a physical event it is brought about by causes within creation, but not by their power alone. Therefore it may not be purely and simply reduced to a natural fact. The miraculous event comes about—also as regards its physical structure—rather through a supernatural intervention by God, as we have just suggested, by showing that it may be seen as a consequence of the incarnation of God's Son. Yet this supernatural influence does not act outside nature, but in it, within it, and uses it as its instrument. The miracle is thus an 'extra-natural' reality, but may also be termed 'intra-natural'. For it is the effect within the creature itself of the supernatural giving of grace, the perfecting of that creature in the design of its own being. The gift of grace to the first human beings thus gave them immortality, and perhaps other related qualities. The grace which consists of the presence in fallen humanity of the incarnate Word can in our view have a similar effect within our nature, manifesting itself in the raising of the dead and the healing of the sick. In this manner it also becomes clear that the miracle refers not arbitrarily but of its very nature to the coming kingdom of God, whose centre is the glorified Christ. But let us not anticipate our reflection on the symbolic function of the miracle, for we have still to reject a second premature conclusion.

It is this: that the miracle is not exceptional. This, also, does not follow from the fact that created causes are active therein. For these causes are not those which function in the usual course of events, and which are at work when the laws of nature hold true. In order to make this clear we must go somewhat more closely into the relation between law and miracle, and develop in more detail some of the incidental remarks we made earlier on this subject (pp. 100–03). Physical laws express a certain constant sort of activity—and a passivity corresponding to this—in material reality and in the human mind in so far as it is dependent upon material reality (hence we have not only mechanical, chemical and biological but also economical and psychological laws). Now, are these laws only schemes into which we fit our many experiences, or is the constant which we ascertain also present independently of our thought?[1] We suggest that the general laws in which we summarise our experience are objective in the same way as our general or universal ideas ('man', 'horse', etc.). Just as universal ideas signify something that is really present in each of the individuals

[1] Here we should like to remark in passing that even the person who sees these laws merely as subjective statements, and who thus adheres to a pure indeterminism, still does not need to consider the miracle as senseless. For in this case it nevertheless remains a phenomenon which rebels against our schemes of thought so that it attracts our attention and can, in a religious context, refer to God. We ourselves, however, would not wish to deny objectivity to the physical laws in such a manner.

to which they apply (individual people. horses), so the general physical law says something about individual cases and is true in each of these individual cases. But just as, on the other hand, universal ideas do not render the whole reality of an individual, so general laws do not give the whole reality of an individual fact.[1] For in the individual fact the general law only holds in a particular manner, indeed, sometimes it does not hold, which is why a

[1] This holds true of general ideas and laws as long as they are being considered on the level of knowledge of the experimental sciences. When philosophy considers these same ideas and laws on its metaphysical level of knowledge, then in our opinion we have a different state of affairs (and we are not alone in thinking this). Knowledge at the level of the experimental sciences uses ideas which simply generalise a sensory datum and which are therefore unequivocally predicated of individual realities, making abstraction of other factors which at the same time determine this individuality ('man' applies in exactly the same way to Peter and John, and makes abstraction of that which makes Peter the individual he is and John the individual he is). Knowledge on a metaphysical level, however, is knowledge of being, being which does not exclude its several specifications but includes them: for nothing falls outside being. Thus this knowledge uses universal ideas as closer definitions of the idea of being, which are therefore, like being, analogously predicated of individual realities, implicitly including their individualising factors ('man' applies analogously, i.e., in the same way and yet at the same time in a different way, to Peter and John and includes that which makes Peter himself and not John, and that which makes John himself and not Peter, as a mode of being human). It appears to us that something similar is the case with the laws of nature and the two levels of knowledge. On the level of the experimental sciences they are unequivocally applied to all the cases they concern, and thus exclude the varying circumstances under which they apply in individual cases, and certainly the exceptions in which they do not. On the metaphysical level these laws are stated analogously, however, and thereby include the individual circumstances in which they hold, and even the exceptions in which they hold true but give way before causes other than those whose existence they indicate. The latter will be borne out by what we now have to say concerning the generality of these laws.

general law says even less about the individual case than the general idea does. Can it therefore still be termed general, or must we say that it expresses that which usually occurs, that it presents no more than a statistical picture of the frequency with which a particular phenomenon takes place? We believe that the latter supposition does an injustice to the generality of the law. Yet on the other hand its generality must not be conceived of in such a way that exceptions are made impossible. One is saying too little when one states that water usually boils at 100°C; and one is saying too much if one states that water boils at 100°C without exception. However, we may avoid both these extremes if we consider the idea of a law in more detail. In the first place a law does not say how something is, but how it should be. This is true of moral and juridical laws; if we accept the same with regard to physical laws then we avoid both difficulties, for then we are saying something that is strictly universal and yet admits exception. Water should boil at 100°C, it tends to do so. In other words there are causes which produce this effect. But they can be hindered in their action by other causes and then we have an exception. In the exceptional case the same cause is still tending to produce the same result as the law indicates, but another cause prevents this. The law is not abolished, but annulled, hindered in its application. Its truth continues to hold, but that truth withdraws before another event.

It is not only in this way that the law holds true in the miracle, however; we may discover two further ways in which the law remains more experimentally recognisable. The first consists in this, that certain boundaries are maintained and that certain processes are rediscovered at a higher level. We see this particularly in the case of miraculous cures. There certain illnesses are suddenly cured, illnesses which can often be cured in a natural way, but then gradually; whereas, for example, no amputated limbs are given back. Yet even this sudden restoration does not simply occur in an indivisible instant (particularly in the case of eye diseases; cf Mk 8:22) and it leaves scars. Taking all things together, the miracle of healing may be characterised as a supernaturally accelerated and extended, indeed, supernaturally forced, natural process of healing. Thus we have an explanation of what was said just previously about the miracle as an extra-natural or intra-natural fact.[1] The second way in which the law is seen to hold in the case of the miracle is that the latter may some-

---

[1] We should like to note, by way of an hypothesis, that even paranormal happenings may be included within certain miracles, but then integrated in a higher power. One might risk a comparison between Jesus' cures from a distance and all sorts of parergic activities of the human body in telekinesis, apparitions, etc. If one and the same sphere of forces were really at play here, then it would be seen even more clearly than in the cases of healing that this natural element is being 'supernaturally forced' or, as we should prefer to say, supernaturally broken open, supernaturally liberated, humanised and taken up into the personality. Such non-miraculous activity often occurs independently of human freedom, it is staged by the unconscious; but Jesus 'perceived in himself that power had gone forth from him' (Mk 5:30 = Lk 8:46). As projections of that unconscious these parergic actions are unbridled and subhuman, products of buried aggression or sexuality; in contrast, the miracle is meaningful and beneficial. The person from whom the above-mentioned activities proceed, the 'medium', is often psychologically unstable, and the activity itself has a disturbing and exhausting effect, of all of which there is no trace in Jesus' miracle. Finally, it must be emphasised that such activity can be a cause by which the influence of Jesus' body may make itself felt at several places, but does not itself provide an explanation of this, of the healing power which goes out from him. In our view this belongs to the world to come, and thereby the miracle is also a revelation of Christ's majesty: 'and the power of the Lord was with him to heal' (Lk 5:17).

times fall among the exceptions foreseen by the law itself. This is so with statistical laws, laws of probability, which say only that a particular process has the greatest or practically the only chance of being realised. This implies, however, that the exceptions also have a chance, even though it may only amount to 1 per cent. It is above all where all the factors in a process are not yet known that the natural sciences are obliged to set up such statistical laws. But since there is always the possibility that other causes should obstruct the action of the cause which makes the law hold, and since the various interactions of nature, as also miracles, are ascertainable facts, for every physical law it may be stated in what percentage of cases it holds, even if this is 99·999 per cent. In such an event the miracle is already contained in the percentage of exceptions that is inherent in the law itself. Thereby it does not cease to be a miracle, however, nor is it reduced to the status of the other exceptions. For it is a miracle through both its exceptional nature and the other elements which make it a sign. Among all the other possible exceptions it is the miracle which bears the signature of its supernatural origin and aim, of which we shall speak presently.

In summary of what we have written concerning this exceptional nature we may say that in doing these miraculous signs in support of his revelation God does not cease to be the creator of heaven and earth. He does no miracle, in our view, by holding back his co-operation with created causes, nor by 'creating something in addition'. It is much more the case that in his miracles the God of wonders remains faithful to his own work of creation by also bringing about the co-operation of created causes, by imparting forces that are active within the plan of nature, by respecting its laws in various ways, even in their exceptions. But all of this does not deny that the miracle is an exception to the law as an objective constant of natural activity. One might call each individual fact in which God's rule speaks to someone a miracle. We, however, shall follow custom in only terming a particular fact a miracle if it is wonderful to all human beings because it constitutes an exception to a law ascertainable by all human beings. Yet a fact does not become that sign which makes it a miracle just through being exceptional. For this other elements are required in addition, and these we shall now discuss.

The atmosphere which surrounds the exceptional fact and makes it into a truly miraculous sign points in two directions: towards the supernatural origin of the miracle, and towards its aim, the confirmation of revelation. Naturally, the same symbolic elements will often refer to both, but in the interests of clarity we shall discuss each of them separately, beginning with those elements which point to the divine origin of the miracle. From what was said above it is evident that for this the exceptional character does not suffice alone. The latter might be purely natural interplay, without any connection with the supernatural. It can also be at the service of demoniacal forces, 'False Christs and false prophets will arise and show signs and wonders, to lead astray, if possible, the elect' (Mk 13:22=Mt 24:24; cf Rev 13:13f.). However, these pseudo-miracles will be surrounded by a sphere of ambiguity, obscurity, unrest, because 'the devil is a liar and the father of lies' (Jn 8:44). Although in his sinfulness man can be attracted by the atmosphere of such a pseudo-miracle, it will come into conflict with the deepest urge of his nature, for that is inwardly orientated towards the salvation that Christ brings (cf pp. 145–9). This conflict brings about an unrest, an ultimate lack of peace after a possible temporary intoxication. In contrast, the authentic miracle, like every other sign of Christ, will present itself in a lasting peace, even if it has startled us at first. Here it is true that 'the peace of God, which passes all understanding, will keep your hearts and your mind in Christ Jesus' (Phil 4: 7).[1] In this way the sphere of the authentic miracle corresponds to an unexpressed desire of our human nature, which God has destined for salvation in Christ. It seems possible, however, to describe this sphere of the authentic miracle in more detail. It speaks with all the more emphasis when we compare it with what we are told of the pagan 'wonder-workers' in the same Hellenistic culture as that in which the gospels were written; for example, the biography of Apollonius of Tyana. We shall then be struck by a threefold characteristic of Jesus' miracles: the unselfishness of their performer, the dignity of the whole event, and its moral-religious purpose.

In the first place, Jesus in unselfish in so far as he never—as Asclepius or Apollonius certainly do—asks a reward for his healing. On the contrary, he also orders his disciples 'Heal the sick, raise the dead, cleanse the lepers, cast out demons. You received without pay, give without pay' (Mt 10: 8). Moreover, in him we see no trace of that self-advertisement at which the pagan mass-healers were such masters. His command of secrecy concerning his miracles and his refusal of signs which are demanded for human motives convinces us of this. Certainly, Jesus asks for faith before or by means of the miracle, faith in himself and thereby self-surrender and worship (see, for example, Jn 9: 35–38), but in the background is his Father, without whom he may do

[1] Cf St Ignatius Loyola's second group of 'Rules for the Discernment of Spirits' in the *Spiritual Exercises*.

nothing (Jn 5: 19), as also the person or persons for whose good the miracle is being done and whose freedom is respected. Christ's miracles are never a powerful trick or a piece of show, but always a good deed and an invitation. They are not performed for an audience, but directed towards a person. This holds true of Jesus' few miracles of nature—for he brings about no signs from the heavens—since he quietens the storm and causes the draught of fish in order to meet his disciples in their own world, so as to lead them subsequently into his: 'henceforth you will be catching men' (Lk 5: 10). It is also noteworthy that Christ's miracles never have the character of vengeance or punishment—he does not wish his disciples to pray for fire from heaven (Lk 9: 54f.) —but always that of help, goodness and forgiveness. Thus we meet an atmosphere not only of human unselfishness, but also of divine beneficence—which is accompanied by the divine dignity we named as a second factor. Publicity and sensation are absent; even more so all the vulgar, theatrical or obscene elements which are repeatedly present in the Greek tales: ridiculous representation of illness, healing in the presence of assistants, by complicated manipulations, by pederasty. With Jesus it is always a clear and simple approach; on only one occasion is there mention of the application of saliva, clay or oil, but usually it is his word alone that achieves the miracle, and often from a distance. Once again we must point to the sphere of divine authority and of faith which expresses itself in prayer—thereby ascertaining at the same time the moral-religious character of the miracle. Not only does the miraculous deed not aim at a show of power, it does not even stop at the healing of the body alone, but is primarily intended for the good of the soul. Basically not only the healing of the paralytic, but all the miracles of Jesus take place 'that you may know that the Son of man has authority on earth to forgive sins'.

It is now seen still more clearly that the two elements in the symbolic function of the miracle which we pointed out besides its exceptional character coincide to a great extent. Much of that which indicates the supernatural origin also refers to the revelation which is confirmed by the miracle. Yet it is worth separately considering this connection of the sign with revelation for a moment. In doing so we should like essentially to contend that there is a direct connection between the two, through which the miracle also becomes a direct sign of revelation, a symbol of its content—and not just a proof that convinces us by means of an argumentation concerning God. The latter would be the case were the symbolic function to consist only of its exceptionality. In such a case one could reason from the miracle thus: here God is working in connection with a doctrine, a message; now God is truthful and thus cannot achieve this work to the advantage of a false teaching; thus the teaching confirmed by the miracle is guaranteed true by God, it is his revelation. As an exception the miracle refers us over and above God's omnipotence to his truthfulness as guarantee for the doctrine. This has certainly come in for ridicule. In this conception God has been compared to an athlete in ancient times who was also a sophist, and who, in order to win authority for the opinions he was presenting, first attempted to demonstrate his athletic ability. Yet this comparison does not hold completely. For in man physical proficiency and mental discernment may exist apart, but in God power, wisdom and truthfulness coincide. But this implies at the same time that the reliability of the teaching need not only be deduced from the miracle by means of a reasoning process.

It can also be evident in a single intuition: God is behind this, 'God has visited his people', without crossing over from one of God's qualities to another. But then other qualities of God will be experienced in the miracle, particularly his love. For let us say it again: the miracle gives not an impersonal demonstration of God's power, but an experience of his saving love. Through this, however, it is also a direct sign of the content of revelation, for this precisely says nothing other than 'God is love' (1 Jn 4: 8, 16). The deeds of goodness which constitute Jesus' miracles give us a pledge for the whole revelation of God's love for men in Christ.

We may go still further and also see the form in which God's love comes to us, the redemption, signified and symbolised in the miracle. We have already heard the Lord himself referring to the forgiveness of sins at the healing of the paralytic and to the advent of God's kingdom at the casting out of the demon. In general his exorcisms and healings point to the decline of the power of sin, to the hour in which 'the ruler of this world shall be cast out' (Jn 12: 31). Jesus' miracles spoke this language for his listeners more than for us; for them the power of the ruler of this world was a reality and illness often or always included a reference to sin (cf Jn 9: 2). Perhaps this is more accurately defined in the case of some ills: thus it is possible that the curing of the haemorrhage—inasmuch as haemorrhage brought with it an impurity (Lev 12: 1–5) which was considered by the prophets as a symbol of sin (e.g., Is 64: 6)—speaks strongly as an announcement of the extinguishing of sin. Conversely, healing was already for the prophets one of the fruits of the messianic salvation; cf Is 35: 5, to which Jesus himself refers Mt 11: 4=Lk 7: 22). If the fathers and seemingly the whole liturgy therefore see in the miracles which Christ wrought during his earthly life a symbol of the work of salvation he now accomplishes through the sacraments, then this vision is certainly not at variance with the general context of the evangelical accounts of miracles. Indeed, we may go further and say even that it is prepared in the gospels, particularly in that of John. For in his story of the man born blind who is sent by Jesus to the pool called Siloam, that is, Healed (Jn 9: 7), we certainly have an allusion to the enlightenment brought by baptism in Christ. The miracle of the multiplication of the loaves refers to the eucharist—probably even in the synoptics, but certainly in John 6, where it is followed by the eucharistic discourse—and perhaps the anointing with oil of the sick by Jesus' disciples (Mk 6: 13) refers to the sacrament of the anointing of the sick (Jas 5: 14). At first we might be inclined to describe this connection between the miracle and the Lord's later works of salvation by the formula: during his earthly life Christ does to the body that which later, glorified in his church, he will do to the soul. However, the fact that healing of the body can be a fruit of the sacrament of anointing the sick, and that it is connected by Paul with the eucharist, even if only in a negative way (1 Cor 11: 30), already warns us against excluding the body from the effects of the sacraments. Nevertheless, the miracles certainly point further: to the restoration of the whole man, with soul and body, at the resurrection. This is in the first place true of Jesus' raising of Lazarus (Jn 11: 21–27). But the other miracles also bring about a restoration (Mk 8: 25; *apekatestē*) which refers to the ultimate 'restoration of all things' (Acts 3: 21 *apokatastasis pantōn*). So we see that the most profound element of the miracle's symbolic function lies in its prefiguration of the whole work of salvation of the glorified Christ, up to his second coming as much as in it. This is the full content of St John's statement that by his signs Jesus 'manifested his glory' (Jn 2:11). Thus the miracle has a teaching function for those who after Christ's glorification look in retrospect at his earthly life. This is why John makes it known several times that the disciples only fully understood Jesus' deeds after his resurrection (e.g., Jn 2:22; 12:16). None the less, this does not remove the fact that already in the time of Jesus' preaching this symbolic element made his miracles demonstrative signs. By giving a preparatory image of the kingdom of God they underlined Jesus' message that it is near at hand, and in proceeding from him they show him as the one who brings it, the Messiah. This was made all the more so in that the people expected God's kingdom to bring with it the resurrection and universal restoration.

Proceeding from the miracle as prefiguration of the future work of salvation of Christ, we may now describe a certain hierarchy among his miracles. The raising of the dead has always counted as the highest of the Lord's miracles. This remains true: it does not, however, need to be based only on their exceptionality, but also and above all on the fact that they most fully represent to us life after the general resurrection. In addition it seems worthwhile to arrange Jesus' miracles around those which are most intimately bound up with him, for he is to be the centre of the new heaven and the new earth. Thus we may firstly group them around Jesus' transfiguration on the mountain. Here also he reveals his glory (Lk 9:32), and in a manner which we expect rather more than that of his other miracles. It is the glory in Jesus' own body that is displayed on Tabor, whilst the other miracles allow us to realise in ourselves the effect of his glory. This central position is

184

perhaps the reason why in the second letter of Peter it is precisely the transfiguration that is named as a guarantee for the Lord's return, confirmed by the prophecies (2 Pet 1: 16–19). Yet the transfiguration also points to another wonder: 'Tell no one the vision, until the Son of man is raised from the dead' (Mt 17: 9).

The glorification on the mountain remains only a fleeting prediction, but Christ's resurrection is the beginning of his majesty, the beginning also of the resurrection of the dead, of the new heaven and the new earth, of the ultimate kingdom in which God is everything in all men. The resurrection is the greatest miracle on account of its exceptionality, but not for this reason alone. In addition to this it is the miracle that stands closest to that which all the miracles prefigure; more, it is even the beginning of it. The resurrection of Christ is a miracle because it occurs in our material world, and therefore has for us the strangeness which, for example, the raising of Lazarus has. But Christ himself already stands in another world. He does not return to this life, like Lazarus or the daughter of Jairus, to die once more —perhaps that is why the Lord calls the first death of both of these a sleep (Mk 5: 32 = Mt 9: 24 = Lk 8: 52; Jn 11: 11)—but he has crossed over, once and for all, to eternal life: 'For we know that Christ being raised from the dead will never die again; death no longer has dominion over him' (Rm 6: 9). The resurrection of Christ is, in a word, not only a miracle, but also itself a secret of faith, which is the reason why Paul does not call our faith without this resurrection a faith without proof, but a faith without content (1 Cor 15: 14; *kenē*).

And so we conclude our description of Jesus' miraculous signs, having given what we believe to be a sufficient exposition of the elements which make the miracle a miracle and thus a sign. We have not attributed this symbolic function only to its exceptional nature but also to other elements which refer on the one hand to the activity of God or those sent by him, and on the other to the revelation which is confirmed by the miracle. In this way the miracle is seen to be an exception to the laws of nature which by virtue of the religious connection in which it arises appears as an act of God in support of his revelation. This definition could also be reversed, by now proceeding not from the exceptional nature, but from the symbolic function of the miracle. We should then say: the miracle is a whole consisting of symbolic elements surrounding revelation, which penetrates even into material reality by making an exception to its laws. In the miracle demonstrative signs materialise themselves into an exception to the laws of nature.[1] Herein we have indicated the actual meaning contained by the miracle. It places us, more so than do Christ's other signs, before the action of God's power (cf the already mentioned scriptural terms *dynameis* and *erga*), because the latter is acting outside the usual forces of nature. It translates the transcendence of God and his revelation into exceptionality. Nevertheless, this exceptionality remains but a single element among the other elements of the symbolic function, and God's power remains always joined with his love.

[1] In the article by Taymans, to which we referred, we should like to single out the following sentences: 'Le miracle est un fait sensible que le cours habituel de la nature n'explique pas, mais que Dieu produit dans un contexte religieux, comme signe du surnaturel' (231). 'Le miracle sert à ponctuer ce dialogue entre l'homme qui doit être sauvé et Dieu Sauveur' (233).

5
Epilogue

As was promised in the introduction, I shall in this epilogue indicate several points on which the preceding chapters require supplementation. It will not be a question of giving a complete elaboration of what has been lacking; that is something I hope to present in a forthcoming book, whenever that can be brought to completion. But the reader is invited in what follows to orientate his thoughts more precisely as regards what has preceded. Perhaps he will get further than I, and then I shall be able to learn from him, as I have learned from many conversations.

Literature

In the preceding chapters I have constantly tried to make holy scripture my point of departure. It was not a question of the ideas of a theological system being subsequently justified with the aid of bibletexts; rather, scripture itself formed the starting-point and gave me my categories. In particular, I discovered the category of the covenant in this way, and believe that I thereby contributed to the view of grace as sublimation with respect to an aspect which had previously remained in the shadow, namely, communion with God himself. On other points, also, I believe I have proceeded from scripture more than is usual, thus, for instance, considering God firstly as God of the covenant and only subsequently as creator, or by presenting the miracle first and foremost as sign, and only thereafter as exception. Yet, looking back, this biblical background retains a somewhat schematic presentation. Of course, a dogmatics work cannot be a collection of exegetical monographs, but today the ideas can certainly be developed in a richer manner. I should like to contribute to this by referring, in connection with certain points, to more detailed publications.

For the fundamental notions of covenant and history reference may be made to Gerhard von Rad's *Theology of the Old Testament* and, on a somewhat more popular level, to the books by H. Renckens: *The Religion of Israel*, and Norbert Lohfink: *Das Siegeslied am Schilfmeer*.[1] In my description of the covenant between God and man I have mentioned God's qualities of 'grace and faithfulness'. The covenant could also be illustrated by God's chief commandment, with its various formulations, and by the relation between grace and law, as it is in two chapters by Lohfink.[2] A chapter by the same author, entitled 'Freiheit und Wiederholung', has points of contact with my section 'The God of history' since, among other things, both pieces contain a reflection

[1] Gerhard von Rad, *Theology of the Old Testament*; H. Renckens, *The Religion of Israel*, London 1967; Norbert Lohfink, *Das Siegeslied am Schilfmeer. Christliche Auseinandersetzungen mit dem alten Testament*, Frankfurt am Main 1965.

[2] N. Lohfink, op. cit., 129–150 ('Das Hauptgebot') and 151–173 ('Gesetz und Gnade'); in more detail: N. Lohfink, *Das Hauptgebot. Eine Untersuchung literarischer Einleitungsfragen zu Deut. 5–11*, Rome 1963.

on Mircea Eliade's *Myth of the Eternal Return* and because Lohfink and I both see a synthesis of linear and cyclic thought in Israel's vision of history. Lohfink has demonstrated the cyclic within the linear more clearly than I by pointing out that the contingent facts of the history of salvation, in particular the exodus and entry, are themselves the form of a mythical enterprise, which is fulfilled again in anamnesis.

In my chapter on creation I have briefly indicated that Israel's faith in creation lies enclosed primarily in its experience of Yahweh's power over its own history and that of the nations. But is only after detailed discussion of Genesis 1 that I have dealt with the rest of the Old Testament. It would have been better to present a more chronological arrangement of the texts in which, for example, the Deutero-Isaiah forms the zenith of the experience of God's creative power in history, Genesis 1 is the fruit of the encounter of this faith with the Babylonian cosmogonies, the wisdom literature the completion of the Old Testament teaching on creation, whilst the New Testament gives Jesus Christ his place therein. Such an account has meanwhile been provided by Paul de Haes: *De schepping als heilsmysterie. Onderzoek der bronnen* (Tielt 1962). That for De Haes creation is not only the condition for salvation, but itself a mystery of salvation, is a point which corresponds with the fact, pointed out by myself, that God's covenant activity can be subsumed under his creation. What I merely indicated is not only developed by De Haes, but is dealt with in more detail by A. Hulsbosch in his book: *God's Creation* (London 1965). Furthermore, I must not fail to mention Henri de Lubac, to whom I owe my view of the relation between nature and grace. When I wrote my text I did not mention him for reasons of security. I can now say openly that therein I was above all inspired by his book *Le surnaturel,* and particularly by his article *Le mystère du surnaturel.* The latter is also the title of a book which once again supports his ideas by a detailed confrontation with the history of theology.[1]

In the chapter on the miracle, its exceptionality is viewed completely and utterly in function of its significatory character. What I said about the notion of 'miracle' continues to be my view. All I would add is that the question of the historicity of the miracle stories has for me become much more complicated than when I wrote this chapter.[2] There I said, 'A creation of belief by the first christian community can no more be the explanation of the originality of the miracle stories than it can be that of the originality of Jesus' whole personality'. I continue to hold the conviction that Jesus' whole personality is no creation of the faith of the community, much rather that the converse may be said to be the case. This personality also makes its mark upon the miracle story and thereby distinguishes the evangelical miracle stories from all others. It remains a question, however, whether this is already sufficient to assure us of their historicity—understood in the modern sense of the word, namely of their having occurred as they are described. Nor would I be any more willing to unconditionally explain the miracle stories on the basis of the community's need to place the person of Jesus over and against the ancient wonderworkers in this respect. A miracle story might arise in a legi-

---

[1] H. de Lubac, *Le Surnaturel. Études historiques,* Paris 1946. Idem, 'Le mystère du surnaturel', in *Recherches de science religieuse,* 36 (1949), 80–121; *The Mystery of the Supernatural,* London 1967.
[2] This is also true of L. Monden's book, *Het Wonder.*

timate way out of such a need, but not necessarily, it seems to me, and certainly not in all cases. In this connection I can refer only with some reservation to the views of Bultmann, in so much as they are partly inspired by a conviction that the miracle presupposes an intervention from without by God, a conviction which in my exposition I was precisely at pains to refute. Apart from this, Bultmann presents us with real questions concerning historicity, questions which, as I see things, can no more be met with a general affirmation than with a general denial. A good dialogue and attempt to find an answer is to be found in an article by L. Bakker: 'Wonderen en ontmythologisering'.[1]

God works through his creatures

In the preceding chapters the relation between created and creator is presented as all-embracing. Not a single part or aspect escapes this relationship, for God's creation consists precisely in his realising everything in the world under all aspects. It was on the basis of this view that I wrote about God's creative activity in relation to his other activities and to the activity of his creature. I remain in full agreement with what I said there. I should even like to put it more forcefully.

It was above all unity that I underlined in the relation between God's creation and his other activities. We must recognise these activities as one, not only in their origin, in God himself, that is, but also in their object, in the world, since everything continues to be from God just as much as its beginning was, and God is as much the generator of secular

[1] See in particular Rudolf Bultmann, 'Zur Frage des Wunders' in *Glauben und Verstehen*, 2nd Aufl., Tubingen, 1954, Bnd I, s. 214–228; L. Bakker, 'Wonderen en ontmythologisering', in *Theologie en Praktijk* 25 (1965), 57–86.

reality in its continuation as he is in its first coming to be. However, I also thought it worthwhile to use the word creation, in contrast with conservation, etc., where something new arises. Here it must also be noted that when I wrote these chapters I certainly wished to leave room for an evolutionary view of the world, but did not give it a positive place in my theology. Later I did in fact do this, as can be seen from other books.[1] Had I done it here, I should have lain even more emphasis on the unity of creation and the other activities and should have subsumed everything under the relationship of creation in a still more radical way. God shows the newness of his creative action by realising our world as a world which is continually renewing itself, or, to use Rahner's phrase, surpassing itself.[2]

I shall, in fact, say something about creation and evolution. For the moment, however, I should like to examine a view in which the lasting nature of the creation relationship comes out very strongly. This view contrasts sharply with that of the working or order-giving creator and might possibly be understood in a pantheistic manner. It is the view of God and world as soul and body, which is to be found even in the writings of Thomas Aquinas.[3] I would rather compare the relation of the creator and the world, ever created by him and ever developing, to that of the human *person* and his body. The point of comparison is that the person is the continual bearer of his body; a bearer, moreover, who on the one hand moves, rules and experiences the body from

[1] P. Schoonenberg, *God's World in the Making*, Pittsburgh-Louvain 1964; Techny, Illinois 1967; Dublin 1965; idem, *Man and Sin. A Theological View*, London-Melbourne and Notre Dame, Ind. 1965; esp. 192–199.

[2] Paul Overhage-Karl Rahner, *Das Problem der Hominisation. Über den biologischen Ursprung des Menschen*, Freiburg 1961, 55–78.

[3] St Thomas Aquinas, *In II Sent.*, dist. 1, q. 1 ad. 1.

within, and yet on the other hand, transcends the body, at least in so far as this person has the freedom to take up his own particular position over and against the conditions of his own body: he can use or abuse health, preserve it or damage it, he can accept sickness and death or harden himself against them in protest; and so on. Similarly, God is the one who continually carries his creation as his own, moves and rules it from within, and expresses himself therein. At the same time he is and remains the transcendent one, who calls and commands the world. The image can fertilise our acknowledgement of the God and Father of Jesus Christ, but it must also be criticised and, if necessary, corrected, by faith in that God. For this reason the biblical image of the working creator and especially that of the commanding creator, together with all the biblical talk about the transcendent God must always accompany this image of person and body. In the wisdom literature the Old Testament has perhaps already found a synthesis between God's transcendence and his all-permeating presence. For on the one hand, wisdom is with God in his heaven and exists before all things, before even the chaos of Genesis 1:1ff, but on the other hand, not only does this wisdom play on earth before the face of God, it also wishes to be with the sons of men (Prov 8:22–31), indeed, it strides across heavens and sea, rules in all peoples, lives and grows in Israel and is made equal with the law (Sir 24). This being at once with God and in creation can be an image, on the one hand of the transcendence of this divine quality and thus of God himself, and on the other of God's immanence in his world through that wisdom which is his emanation, the expansion of his person.

The image of person and body expresses another aspect of the relation between creator and creature particularly well, namely that the creator realises his creature in its own activity. When someone freely moves his arm, the movement of that arm is both completely the result of his freedom and completely caused by biochemical processes, without the two competing. Such is also the case between God and world, God and man: when humans are more active this does not imply a lessening of God's initiative, but on the contrary, an increase in it; it does not exclude God's initiative, but is the consequence of it. This has already been dealt with sufficiently in the preceding chapters. Here I should like to add that the thesis developed there holds not only in a positive manner, but also exclusively. The activity of the creature in no sense stands in the way of God's activity, which is why we may say of God that, once his creation is given, he works in it only by making created causes active. He has and is the continual initiative, but he does not intervene or interpose in the sense of wholly or partly excluding created causes and then filling their vacant places himself. God leads and activates this world in its continual self-transcendence, but fills no gaps and adds nothing to the world purely from without.

The exclusive part of my thesis, which remained in the shadow in preceding chapters and is being explicitly added here, demands a more detailed proof. One might already attempt to draw a proof out of the realisation that God must always remain God, always transcendent. Well, one might contend, he is no longer this to the extent that he replaces a created cause: for then he is inserting himself in the chain of limited causes, placing himself within the categories of the world, and ceasing thereby to be transcendent. The question is, however, cannot God replace a limited cause in an eminent way, without himself taking on limitation? Certainly, the question is likely to return under another form: does this eminent replacement not, in its turn, mean the introduction of an intramundane reality? And from the point of view of God's incarnate Word an affirmative answer becomes very likely; but for the moment let us leave this question undecided. It is better to prove the point positively by showing that every activity of God takes up within itself the activity of the creature, or, in other words, realises itself by making creatures themselves active. This we may do in four steps, which partially overlap.

1 Let us begin with God's immanence, presented above in the image of the creator as the person who bears, animates and experiences his creation. Whenever God acts towards his creation, he nevertheless always acts as the God who is immanent *in* his creation. Because of God's transcendence we can say that his activity takes place 'from outside', but because of his immanence we must also immediately add that he also acts 'from within' (and from this it is obvious that this opposition is relative, as is that between 'vertical' and 'horizontal', and that of all spatial images in relation to God). What, however, is the meaning of this action by God from outside? If it has any real meaning, then it is that it involves creatures and itself makes them active.

2 God's activity perfects his creation. This means that this activity, precisely as the activity of God, does not exclude creatures, much rather that it includes them; indeed, we might say: it includes them maximally. To be sure, this does not necessarily mean to say that every creature is involved in each of God's actions. But it does mean that the exclusion of a creature finds its grounds not in God, but in the activity of other creatures. (Competition only arises

between creatures, mutually, or more accurately, between creatures in the measure of their materiality; not between God and creature.) Indeed, the fact that God's activity perfects means that it involves creatures each according to their own capacity.

3 The latter can also be affirmed when being created is seen as a participation, a sharing in the being of the creator. This seems a very abstract point of departure, but it was my intention precisely to remove the abstract character of the notion of 'participation'. Every creature participates in its own way in God's being, but then in God's concrete being. Not only in a 'metaphysical essence', in a fullness of being conceived of by us, but in the concrete creating God who continually realises the world. Thus also in God's continued creation. Every creature participates in its own manner in God's creative activity with respect to all creatures (all other creatures, but also himself: in the manner proper to his own level of being the creature is *causa sui*). Thus, in his own manner and within his own limited possibilities the creature always has a part in the realisation of his fellow creatures: to this same degree he is involved by the creator in his continual creation.

4 Finally, this insight is once more confirmed when, thinking completely in terms of the world, one reflects upon its unity. This unity brings with it that all intramundane beings also participate in each other, are with and in each other: this finds its highest realisation in the fact that on the one hand the world enters into our consciousness and that on the other our insights and our freedom enter the world by giving it its ultimate meaning. This also means, however, that creatures realise each other in so far as they possess the capacity to do so, or con-

versely: that creatures exist through and from each other. Certainly, there continually arise realities that are really new. But with all their novelty they are never completely strange to the rest of creation, with which they do, after all, constitute one world. Thus a new reality does not enter the world purely from without, it must also, in some way or another, be *from* the world. Which in turn means the same as: that which God creates as something new is at the same time brought forth by intramundane causes. Or to put this in a more active fashion: the creator involves the other creatures whenever he realises something new.

Evolution, hominisation, history

The considerations presented above are fundamental to our theological talk of the world as evolving. As mentioned, in the preceding chapters I have merely left room for such a conception, but have not integrated it into my theology. This I should now like to do, and have already made a start in my book *God's World in the Making*. I am thereby following in the footsteps of Pierre Teilhard de Chardin, who was, as Jean Guitton puts it, the prophet, but not the master of a theological vision of evolution.[1] I do not wish to bind myself to the details of Teilhard's views, but together with him I think I am able to see the whole of the visible world as involved in one total evolution. The unity of this universe is the reason for also accepting the issuing forth of the various realities out of each other, and this following the time course in which they appeared. According to this view the lower beings precede the higher and thus, generally speaking, the higher arise out of the lower (where the ideas of

[1] Jean Guitton, 'Le phénomène Teilhard', in *Informations catholiques internationales*, 3 (1961), 28f.

'lower' and 'higher' rest upon an intuitive insight which does not easily admit of being assessed against a generally accepted criterion). In the preceding consideration it was precisely made clear that the distinction between higher and lower beings, even if it may be rightly termed a distinction of essence, is not in contradiction with a real issuing of higher from lower being. That all that comes into being must have a sufficient basis is true even within creation. That this basis may not be 'less' than what comes forth from it, however, is a presupposition which excludes all evolution *a priori*. In the conception, sketched above, of creation as a participation in the reality of God it is rather the opposite that is to be expected. For then God is the reality which completely possesses its own sufficient ground, so much so that it *is* its own ground; the other beings have sufficient grounds only in a derived sense, in their own order at least, for their ultimate ground is God. But, once again, not in the sense that from without God supplements the created ground of the creature along its own lines; in other words, not in the sense that in the evolution of a higher being he 'contributes by creation' that which has been lacking so far. No, God is not the missing piece of intramundane ground, he is the ground and cause of the whole world precisely in its evolving, continually surpassing itself anew. He realises the world 'out of nothing', out of himself, as a world in which one thing really comes forth out of another, the higher from the lower. God is always greater, transcending precisely by realising a world that surpasses itself.

Philosophically and theologically, the most interesting event of evolution is hominisation. It also appears to be the greatest jump in evolution, for the latter seems to consist not only in the continual appearance of higher beings, but also in that these higher beings, in the measure that they are higher, arise through ever greater jumps. Nevertheless, there is also a continuity here, a real issuing forth of the higher out of the lower, a real transition. This is revealed, perhaps, in the fact that the enormous jump from animal to man took place in a lengthy and biological cultural transition which was difficult to notice. God is active and creating even in hominisation; nor is this by adding a reality from outside, but by making his whole creation execute this greatest of all forms of self-surpassing in the primate branch. This is expressed by seeing the human body as the product of evolution and thus of God's mediate creation, whilst the soul is supposed to be immediately created by God. Objections may be made against this formulation, however. The distinction between mediate and immediate is precisely not applicable to God's creation. One can speak of mediate creation in so far as God works through his creatures, but not in the sense in which he might be thought to stand in a row of causes, not even when he is thought of as the first of them. His influence is not screened off by intermediate links and only subsequently passed on; no, he is immediately present in his creatures, active and immediately creating. Therefore the body and soul of man are both as much the mediate as the immediate creation of God. The body stems from the evolution in which God has been creating immediately, and the soul that was immediately created by God does not stand outside evolution in so far as this has man as its terminus. This last remark demands a more detailed explanation, which can only be given after we have also made a critical examination of the distinction between soul and body. In thomistic philosophy body and soul are not parts of man which can be separated over and against each other. For the body has the soul as its inward principle of life (as opposite pole to the material principle or *materia prima*), and thus the soul is immanent in the body, yet at the same time transcends it. Perhaps the relation is expressed better when one talks of *person* and body, although the soul is not simply the person, but the principle of personal existence. It is precisely as a person that man transcends his body and thereby also the influence of all causes within the world. Every being that is caused or brought forth is at the same time more than purely the product of its causes; it is itself, it exists 'outside' its causes. In this way the living being is more than the fruit of its parent-beings, it lives and moves itself. Man is certainly more than the product of his parents, he is completely their child, and yet, precisely as a person, independent of them, free with regard to them (sometimes in a struggle which shows, in its turn, just how much he is a product of them). Thus, if we wish to draw a distinction between body and person (or soul as the principle of personal existence), then we may say that both are completely God's creation, and immediately so, but that only man as a person (or man considered as a soul) is *exclusively* God's creation. And so God is not the creator of just a part which might be supposed to proceed from him immediately, but *also* the creator of the whole man (and of every being) *in so far* as he does not arise from other causes. From what has been said previously it will be clear that all this holds not just for the men who first came from primates, but for every human being.

A question which is going to be of importance for the meeting between faith and an evolutionary world-view is that concerning the necessity of evolution up to and including man. That it takes place under God's creative activity says nothing about its contingency or necessity: God's government does not exclude intramundane accident, nor is his freedom in contradiction with the realisation of a necessarily-running process. Therefore this question will have to find its answer in the sciences and in philosophical reflection upon the data they provide. The answer, which I do not feel competent to give, will play a part in the answering of another question which is today beginning to attract more and more attention, namely whether there is life, and human life, elsewhere in the universe. When it is established that the million or so galaxies, of whose existence we can be certain, each consists of a number of solar systems, and that there is a chance that in these countless solar systems there might be planets which are subject to conditions comparable to those of the earth, then the question of (human) life on those planets is reduced to the question whether or not (human) life develops necessarily (or with what necessity and what contingency) when once the conditions are given. And if the possibility of planets inhabited by human beings impresses itself upon our thought, questions arise concerning an eventual economy of salvation for those beings and, thereby, concerning our own. To be sure, such questions will have to be asked, should we ever make contact with such beings; however, they are also becoming more real in the measure that the existence of these beings is changing from mere possibility into a serious hypothesis. Meanwhile, the attention of our theology remains directed mainly towards the human beings of this earth.

One more point must be made with respect to evolution and us humans; namely that evolution does not cease with the appearance of man, that it proceeds further in the most radical way precisely in human history. This is the most valuable insight in

Teilhard's vision. He deserves even more praise for his speculations concerning the fulfilment of evolution in man and in its hominised continuation than for those concerning evolution before the appearance of life. But at the same time it is perhaps Teilhard's greatest weakness that he did not sufficiently bring out the essential element of this hominised evolution. Hominised evolution is history. The new element which appears in human history is the freedom and responsibility of man: a freedom that is always situated and is even continually seeing itself limited by determinisms, but—therefore—a freedom nevertheless. Therefore statistical laws hold also in human history, but they register the activity of a freedom which in its turn can break them. Or to say the least: a freedom which inwardly assimilates all situations and all determinism in loving acceptance or in rebellious refusal. Thus there is room for grace in human history and room for a reply to it of faith or sin.

This freedom works itself out in the domination of the intra-human world, but above all in the relation of human being to fellow human being. In the former relationship it is more a human being's insight, skill and power which are in play, and not so much his freedom: a discovery cannot be resisted, it would seem, and its use, given that this is economical, certainly cannot. Freedom only begins to become really visible when it is a question of the application of our power over each other and of community with each other. Here is revealed the goal of evolution as a whole and of human history in particular: a community of love that binds together as many human beings as possible. What is being formulated here on the basis of man is what God offers us as his covenant and his kingdom. Creating, giving grace and redeeming us from our refusal, he wishes therein to unite human beings with himself and with one another, granting them the possibility of love, which is at the same time love of God and love of one's fellow men. God does this completely in human history, which he thereby makes into a history of salvation for those who accept his kingdom. He does this definitively in Jesus Christ, who is thereby a terminus to God's partial giving of salvation—the definitive Word after he had spoken 'in many and various ways' (Heb 1:1)—but who is at the same time the definitive unleashing, the indestructible beginning of a new humanity, and who, as both together, is as 'the last Adam' (1 Cor 15:45).

Nature and grace

When there is mention of 'grace', there is a need to talk of its supernatural character. In the preceding chapters this has been done in detail. Here two further questions may be posed, concerning the actual distinction between nature and grace, as such, and concerning the application to grace of the principle that God works through his creatures.

In the preceding chapters two reasons have already been pointed out which make the distinction between nature and grace difficult, if not impossible, to discern. The first is that grace is personal communion with God, which includes a perfection of the creature itself, thus in the creature itself, thus a created perfection or mode of being. Hence this element in the giving of grace falls under creation. I have developed this by saying that God's creative activity includes his covenant. A second reason why the distinction between grace and nature is difficult to point out lies in nature's openness to grace, a point on which I have followed de Lubac and continue to do so. If human 'nature', or that reality which belongs to the essence of man, is a question and an openness orientated towards grace, then this human reality itself will in its turn be different according to whether it is or is not, is more or less, 'satiated' with grace. This becomes even more clear when one remembers that man is essentially, in his deepest reality, a person, and that a person is a freedom (and not only has freedom), a freedom which can change not only the world around itself and its own corporeality, but also, and in particular, gives itself an attitude and thus determines its own fate. Hence the human person determines himself first and foremost through encountering God's grace, as it is offered him here and now, with acceptance or refusal.

The evolutionary and historical view I have developed in this epilogue adds a third reason to the two reasons why it is difficult to define the distinction between grace and nature. The reality known as human 'nature' is not permanent, but is itself in evolution. Precisely in as much as it is personal in its deepest essence, it always exists in history and determines itself with respect to every gift of grace, in which determination it is continually encountering new gifts of grace. Thus one might say that today's 'nature' or person is yesterday's grace. Just as today a man experiences the giving of grace as an offer and a gift over and against himself, and therefore as something distinguished from his 'nature', so he is already existing through previous grace and the reply he has given it. I therefore feel able to say that the distinction between nature and grace is to be defined in a purely formal way, and that the content of such a definition is continually altering. The distinction is but the objective reflection of the fact that grace is always grace, gift, answer to our request, and not an object due by our own right or a product of our own capability. The theological and magisterial contention that nature and grace are distinct must be interpreted in function of this datum of revelation concerning God's giving and selection, and not conversely. The distinction between nature and grace is an interpretation and a conclusion, the point of departure having been gift and singling out by God. The conclusion may not be used in order to deduce further conclusions which in their turn define the starting-point itself. Here we have come upon a hermeneutic principle which is of wide application in theology. Cases in which its applicability probably ought to be investigated are: the doctrine of sacramental marks in connection with the unrepeatibility of three of the sacraments; the doctrine of original sin, in connection with infant baptism; pre-existence and virgin birth, in connection with Jesus' divine sonship.

In this way our thesis that God's bestowal of grace belongs to his creation is strengthened by the insight that, whilst preserving their formal distinction, a boundary cannot in practice be drawn between nature and grace. However, the fact that the gifts of grace fall under creation establishes at the same time that the principle developed above, of God's working through his creatures is also applicable to his work of grace or covenant activity. The only question is: how must it be expressed in more detail? In addition, one must remember here that God does not just work through another creature, but, as I have pointed out, also creates every creature as a *causa sui* in its own way, as something realising itself. In his life of grace God stands before us as a God of covenant, as our Thou. Hence he can only encounter us in a created Thou, in a fellow human being, and he does this in the most sublime manner in Jesus Christ, the man who is his Son. For how can the God who is immanent *in* everything and works from within stand *over and against* me except in another? God freely loves us by approaching us with gifts in the other person, and this giving can even lie concealed in a prayer for help, for even the person who approaches me with a request bestows his company upon me. But this is not to deny that God also places me in a giving relationship to others, gives me inward capabilities for this which do not come by way of others but precisely supplement those of others. This God does by inwardly raising me above my own powers and demands in the created gifts of grace which have already been discussed above. Such gifts are also granted me through the other person: his help, his word, witness, his part in dialogue and sacrament, also grant me an enrichment which is not merely external, which is an inward gift of grace, an actual grace, or, bound up with influences which affect the whole of my life, an habitual grace. But God also develops me as a person from within, by actual and habital gifts of grace without the mediation of others. In its turn, however, this personal presence of God which acts from within directs me towards the other person. And so God gives himself to me in the other, but also to the other in me; hence he gives himself by giving us to one another, he is our 'Thou' by making us 'we' in and around Christ; he is our Father, as we may say because of Christ.

Miracles

Now that I have gone through the main theses of the preceding chapters, it rests only for me to say a brief word about miracles. I began by subsuming these under the category of sign and have made their exceptional character completely subordinate to and taken up by their significatory character. The miracle is not only striking and astonishing to the beholder

206

who sees the course of nature interrupted, it awakes an astonishment by which a person feels addressed; indeed, it is a punctuation mark in God's conversation with man.[1] I should like to emphasise, even more firmly than before, that this exceptional character is no intervention from without, no removal of the forces of creation, but a heightened involvement, in which its completion is precisely made manifest. Moreover, it may be stated, and in a manner even more simple than that in the relevant chapter, that the laws are not abolished, but taken up into a higher order; just as, for example, gravity remains but is overcome in a plant that grows upwards. The physical causes whose activity is indicated by physical laws continue of themselves to be oriented towards that activity, but this is taken up into the biological, the biological in turn into the psychological, and so on—and, as has already been suggested, I should be inclined to add: the psychological is taken up and receives its form in a human being's believing reply, so that in turn the psychological influences the biological. Under this aspect there is a parallel with the so-called moral miracles, which constitute a part of every miraculous sign and which appear to be *the* miraculous signs for our times, the intrinsically christian or New Testament miracles. In this sort of miracle statistical laws are taken up in a higher force of love. According to statistical laws good decisions only gradually gain the upper hand, usually when at the same time they also have the support of prestige and advantage, just as a physical miracle accelerates this slow and difficult process by, for instance, elevation into an event of psychological liberation through contact with

[1] F. Taymans, 'Le miracle, signe du surnaturel', in *Nouvelle Revue théologique*, 77 (1955), 225–245; 'Le miracle sert à ponctuer ce dialogue entre l'homme qui doit être sauvé et Dieu Sauveur.'

God's love, so also a moral wonder is the taking up and thereby the overcoming of statistical law, once again by a redeeming love, which is now not only received, but also given or imitated.

Having thus described the significatory and exceptional character of the miracle, we also find an attitude when we encounter the miracle stories, particularly those in the gospels. I have already said that these stories need to be investigated in more detail as regards their historicity, in the current sense of that term, and that, once more, I do not feel competent to do this myself. Every investigator, whether he be 'progressive' or 'conservative', has his presuppositions, which he corrects through eventual contact with the data; everyone proceeds from an anticipatory conception, a *Vorverständnis* as Bultmann puts it, of which it is to be hoped that it does not become a prejudice. Once we have purified our idea of the miracle of all thoughts of an additional creation or an intervention from without, an exclusion of created causes, a cancellation of laws, we are left with an expectation, and that a limited one, concerning encounter with a miracle. Such an anticipatory notion can be summarised in a few short points. (1) Because a miracle is precisely not an intervention or exclusion, there is no reason to deny in advance the occurrence of miracles. (2) The extraordinary is at all times to be expected from God. For he is the one 'who by the power at work within us is able to do far more abundantly than all that we ask or think' (Eph 3: 20). Since the miracle is not a contradiction, it may not form an exception to this expectation. (3) On the other hand, this same conception of the miracle will also limit our expectation. In the first place we expect God to lead (and fulfill) his creatures along their own ways, to remain faithful to the laws of his own creation, which are revealed primarily in the normal course of things. An indication in this direction is the fact that the result of the miracles recounted in the New Testament is something completely usual: health, normal life (so movingly sketched in the story of the former demoniac in the land of the Gerasenes, Mk 5: 15f.). (4) Even in the exceptional case constituted by the miracle, an involvement rather than an exclusion of intramundane factors is to be expected. An exclusion does not follow from the fact that God is active, but from the fact that other created forces are brought in. (5) It is therefore not at all rationalism, rather healthy theology, to attempt to point out such forces at play in miraculous events, certainly on a general level; for example, by saying that one rather expects miracles which take place on the basis of the human personality and its existence in a human body (one's own or those of others who are connected with one), than in inanimate nature. (6) Finally, it is to be remembered that all God's activity is directed towards our salvation and that the miracle co-operates in the announcing of that salvation. On the contrary, the calamity which follows sin is not contributed by God, but is the product of sin itself in its own order (and is, of course, from God in so far as God realises this combination of cause and effect). Therefore it is not the punishing miracle but the miraculous deed of salvation that is to be expected historically, which is in harmony with the fact that the gospels narrate only miracles of salvation. With this we have sketched an anticipatory conception and an expectation with which one may approach the accounts of miracles. It may not be allowed to become a prejudgement or an *a priori* denial, for our thought concerning possibilities and impossibilities is regulated by the message directed towards us, not vice versa.

In this epilogue I have given further sharpness and depth to the chapters translated from the first two volumes of my dogmatics work. My insight concerning evolution has expanded and my views on the distinction between nature and grace have become more supple; my most fundamental views, however, have developed along the same line throughout. And yet this whole oeuvre is still incomplete, for all this thought concerning intercourse between God and man demands fulfilment and completion in a thought-out acknowledgement of the God-man, in christology. Only in God's Word, which is completely and wholly human, will these considerations find their ultimate criterion: by the fact of Jesus Christ they are either denied or affirmed and completed. But they also provide an introduction to the understanding of Christ: they offer no prejudgement, but they do offer an anticipatory view. And for this reason I am happy to be able to publish them now in English.

Index